This

The Burston Rebellion

Betka Zamoyska

Betka Zamoyska is the author of *Elizabeth I*, published in 1981 by Longmans in the UK and by McGraw-Hill in the States. She is a graduate of Lady Margaret Hall College, Oxford. After leaving university she worked as a journalist and, for three years, was a television preview critic for *The Sunday Times*. She is now a researcher for the BBC and a freelance writer.

For Norman

THE BURSTON REBELLION

BETKA ZAMOYSKA

ARIEL BOOKS

BRITISH BROADCASTING CORPORATION

I would like to thank Ruth Caleb and Norman Stone, with whom I worked on the film of *The Burston Rebellion*. Without their help and cooperation this book would never have been written. I am also enormously grateful to Stephen Peet for allowing me to use the transcripts from his 'Yesterday's Witness' programme; to Eileen Atkins for writing such an entertaining foreword; to Alun Howkins for his specialist knowledge of the Norfolk unions; to José Cannell who spent her weekends typing the manuscript; to Susan Kennedy who has taken such care in the editing of this book and particularly to Bertram Edwards who allowed me to look at his research papers and documents and who has written the epilogue, which brings this story up to the present time.

Betka Zamoyska 1985

The publishers would like to thank the Trustees of the Burston School Strike Fund for permission to quote extensively from *The Burston Rebellion* by Tom Higdon, and to Basil Blackwell and Sons for the use of extracts from *Hooligans and Rebels* by Stephen Humphries; and the following for the use of their photographs: Bertram Edwards, pages 65, 66, 67, 68, 69, 75 (bottom), 76, 78 (top); the Trustees of the Burston Strike School Fund, pages 70, 71, 72, 73, 74, 75 (top); Win Potter, page 77; Tony Timmington, pages 78 (bottom), 79; BBC Radio Times (Don Smith), page 80.

First published 1985

Published by the British Broadcasting Corporation
35 Marylebone High Street, London WIM 4AA

ISBN 0 563 20389 7

Contents

Foreword *by Eileen Atkins*   7

1   The Years at Wood Dalling   9

2   Early Days at Burston   20

3   The Union and the Farmers   29

4   The Parish Council Elections   39

5   Official Inquiry – and Dismissal   48

6   'We Want our Teachers Back'   57

7   The School on the Green   85

8   A Village at War   96

9   'A Hall of Freedom'   103

Epilogue *by Bertram Edwards*   109

Selected reading list   117

It's a long way to Burston Station,
It's a long way to go,
It's a long way to Burston Station
To catch the train we know.
Goodbye Little Willie,
Farewell Kaiser Bill,
It's a long way to Burston Station
But we're all on Strike still.

Foreword

When I first met Norman Stone and Ruth Caleb, the director and producer of the BBC television film, *The Burston Rebellion*, to discuss its making, I had never heard of the school strike that had taken place in Norfolk in 1914. I took away a script to read and found it such a heartening and moving story that I was thrilled when they asked me to play the part of Kitty Higdon, the school teacher at the centre of the conflict. Having established that Tom Higdon, Kitty's husband, was to be played by Bernard Hill, an actor I liked and admired, my next question was to ask who were going to play the schoolchildren. 'We've cast them,' said Norman. 'They're all local kids and they're absolutely terrific.'

And they were! From the first day that I entered the classroom dressed as Mrs Higdon and Norman introduced me to my class, I fell in love with them. Children pass in and out of fantasy more easily than adults – they have no difficulty in pretending to be someone else – but some of the younger ones, I think, really believed I was a kind of teacher, and what was real to them and what wasn't became a little blurred in the filming. I always arrived on the set very early in the morning – although I wore very little make-up for the part, I had to put on a wig and layers of clothes, and that can take a long time. By the time the children arrived I was always dressed and bewigged, and I'm certain that many of them thought that is how I always looked. Even though they knew that they themselves had to put on special 'old-fashioned' clothes for the film, it didn't seem to occur to them that I would do the same!

Five-year-old, red-headed William (who looked just like Just William) pulled and tugged at his collar incessantly. 'You won't have to wear it much longer, William,' I said one day when he was pulling at it quite desperately. 'How much longer, Mrs Higdon?' he asked pathetically. 'By the time you've counted to a hundred, then you can take it off,' I said, thinking we must have got the shot in by then. Halfway through the next take I saw William mouth 'One hundred', and off came the collar, with a great sigh of relief, and on to the floor. Luckily the camera was on me.

One of the difficulties of filming with children is to prevent them from looking into the camera. Norman would say to them. 'Now, no matter what happens you must not take your eyes away from Mrs Higdon. You must keep looking at her all the time.' Another five-year-old, Andrew, took this as a challenge. He would swivel his head from side to side as far as it would go and then try to turn his head upside down, but he always kept his eyes on me. This made me laugh so much I often found it difficult to keep my mind on what I was doing. If any of the children weren't concentrating during a take I would often throw in a line to them: 'Come on, Polly, sit up straight,' or, 'Stop doing that Nicholas, it isn't very funny.' Which was all right when the child concerned was called Nicholas, or William or Andrew, but I had to be very careful to get the right period name. It would have ruined a take if I'd said 'Samantha, please take your finger out of Jason's ear', or 'No, Wayne, we don't *all* want to see what a long tongue you have,' and, yes, I did often feel like Joyce Grenfell!

Bernard and I became so involved in our parts that we started to prepare lessons to teach the children between takes – we told ourselves that it was to keep them amused, but actually it was because we loved the rapport we had with them. It also made the playing of our characters so much easier because the children really seemed to accept us as teachers.

After we'd shot the scene where Kitty and Tom say goodbye to the children as they are forced to leave the school after their dismissal by the Board of Managers, one seven-year-old girl came up to me, almost weeping, and asked if she would ever see me again.

'Yes,' I said, 'because the story is that you go on strike now, so Mr Higdon and I don't leave after all.'

'So you're not really going,' she said, and I could tell that for her the story and reality had become merged.

Eileen Atkins

Chapter 1
The Years at Wood Dalling

Dare to be a Daniel,
Dare to stand alone,
Dare to have a purpose true,
Dare to make it known.

On January 31st, 1911, at dusk, two solitary individuals, a woman and a man, were observed walking through the fairy village of Burston, coming from the direction of Diss. Pretty as the village is with its windmill, its bridge over the stream, its pink-washed cottages, its slopes, patches of green and plantation, and with, of course, its less beautiful spots of housing dilapidation and its church without a tower, the strangers appeared to take little notice of its scenery. They had done a four or five-mile tramp from Diss railway station, the train from Norwich having taken them through the Burston station without stopping, as it has a habit of doing.

In his autobiographical account of the events that were soon to disrupt the life of this remote Norfolk village, Tom Higdon describes his first impression of Burston, where he and his wife Kitty were being sent as teachers to the village school.

Tom was a broad-built man with an outgoing manner that could switch from aggressive and bombastic to easy-going and kind. At forty-two, he was five years younger than his wife and, unlike her, was not originally from the professional classes. He was born in 1869 at East Pennard in Somerset where his father Dennis was a farm labourer. His mother Ann signed the birth register by making a mark. On 4 July 1896 Tom married Annie Catherine Schollich (Kitty). The marriage certificate records his occupation as 'teacher' and hers as 'schoolmistress'.

Kitty was a small, brusque woman with a determined chin and bright, boot-button eyes. Her father had been a shipwright and her family were said to have been Austrian aristocrats who had fled to England for political reasons at the beginning of the nineteenth century. Unlike Tom, she had been fully trained as a professional teacher. She evidently had had a better education, and she also had the advantage of other accomplishments. She could speak French, play the piano, and sing beautifully, but her skills did not extend to domesticity. A pacifist, she was also a vegetarian as a matter of principle and seldom bothered to cook. She would neglect the washing-up in favour of a long country walk and her pupils often came to wash-up for her when a week's worth had accumulated (Kitty always paid them for this and any other domestic tasks). The Higdons lived mainly on a diet of bread and cheese with occasional 'treats' produced by women in the village who would send their children over to the Schoolhouse with a cauldron of soup or a freshly baked pie.

Tom was only a certificated teacher which meant that he had probably received a training through the pupil-teacher system. This was one of the few ways in which sons of labourers could stay on at school and receive some form of secondary education. Brighter pupils were selected to help the teacher and, in return, they received a rudimentary type of teacher training and were allowed some time to pursue their studies. A Government report of 1839 describes a pupil teacher as:

> A young teacher, in the first instance introduced to the notice of the Master by his good qualities, as one of the best instructed and most intelligent of the children; whose attainments and skill are full of promise; and who, having consented to remain at a low rate of remuneration in the school, is further rewarded by being enabled to avail himself of the opportunities afforded him for attaining practical skill in the art of teaching, by daily practice in the school, and by gratuitous superintendence of his reading and studies by the Master, from whom he receives lessons on technical subjects of School instruction every evening.

Both the Higdons were strong-willed and independent-minded, and yet their marriage was a remarkably happy one. They seldom quarrelled and their loyalty to each other never wavered. They both shared the same strong Christian faith, based on a literal belief in the Bible, and as Christian Socialists, their reforming zeal sprang from the knowledge that all men were equal in the sight of God and should be treated equally.

Kitty had been brought up as a member of the Church of England but Tom was a Primitive Methodist and a lay preacher. The Primitive Methodists, a democratic sect, encouraged their members to preach the Gospels. Their chapels were centres of political as well as religious activities (in the 1870s and '80s many of the early meetings of the farm labourers' unions were held in the chapels and they were important training grounds for trade union members whose formal education was over by the age of fourteen). As the Rector of Scarning in Norfolk wrote in 1886:

> Explain it how we will, and draw our inferences how we choose, there is no denying it that in hundreds of parishes in England the stuffy little chapel by the wayside has been the only place where for many a long day the very existence of religious emotion has been recognised; . . . the only place where the peasantry have enjoyed the free expression of their opinions, and where, under an organisation elaborated with extraordinary sagacity, they have kept up a school of music, literature and politics unaided by dole or subsidy – above all, a school of eloquence in which the lowliest has become familiarised with the rules of debate, and has been trained to express himself with directness, vigour and fluency.

Tom's political motivation may well have grown out of his childhood experiences as the son of a Somerset labourer at a time when the old paternalism between master and man was being replaced by a more ruthless system of hiring casual labour to meet the fluctuating demands of farm life. Many labourers were laid off in the winter months when there was no work for them and this floating labour force was a constant threat to those in regular employment. It was only when Joseph Arch helped to set up the first branch of the Agricultural Labourers' Union in Warwickshire in 1872 that the labourers dared to demand a fair day's wage for a fair day's work. News of Arch's union soon spread to other counties and in the early summer of 1872 Arch attended a large union meeting in Somerset on Ham Hill, not far from East Pennard where Tom grew up. The struggles of those early unions to establish rights for the agricultural labourers may well have left an impression on an intelligent boy like Tom.

Before they came to Norfolk, the Higdons lived in London. Tom was an assistant master at St James's and St Peter's School, Piccadilly, a Church of England school in the poor quarter of Soho. In August 1901, the headmaster's testimonial stated that:

> Mr Higdon has worked in the above school to my satisfaction during the past two years and you will find him an energetic and conscientious teacher.

He has taken the First and Second Standards comprising 60 boys and has loyally carried out any suggestion which I have offered him.

I can only add that I shall be sorry to lose him.

I am, Yours Truly, W. H. Atkinson.

When they first entered the village of Burston, the Higdons were in low spirits. They had not wanted to take up their teaching posts at the Council School and had almost handed in their notice. For over eight years they had been teaching at another Norfolk school in the village of Wood Dalling, about 40 miles from Burston. In spite of good reports from the School Inspectors about their work, the Higdons had been dismissed because of 'friction' between them and the School Managers. The School Managers' Board, which consisted of the parson and local farmers, wanted to put a stop to Tom's political activities. He had helped to set up a local branch of the Agricultural Labourers' Union. The first Norfolk unions, which had sprung up in the wake of Arch, had split into factions and eventually petered out. A new network of local unions was gradually being established.

Kitty had campaigned for better conditions in the school, which was ill-lit and had inadequate heating and sanitation. As Tom recalled: 'Practically a new school, at a cost of £400 or £500 was built by the Education Committee as a direct result of her agitations.'

Another source of friction between the Higdons and the farmers on the Managers' Board was the illegal employment of children during school hours. The farmers of Wood Dalling, as generally at the time, were used to employing children as casual labour for jobs such as clearing stones, bird scaring, gleaning, particularly in the busy seasons, and it never occurred to them that there was anything wrong in taking the children out of school; Tom Higdon thought differently. Things came to a head when he caught Farmer Gamble employing one of his pupils to lead a drill horse in a field opposite the school room. When Farmer Gamble stood his ground and refused to let the boy go back to his lessons, Tom Higdon went for the farmer and was afterwards charged with assault. The *Norwich Mercury* of 16 November 1902 gives a blow by blow account of the incident:

A stranger case of assault than that investigated at Reepham Petty Sessions on Monday rarely comes before a bench of Norfolk Magistrates. Thomas Higdon, schoolmaster, of Wood Dalling, was summoned for assaulting Henry Gamble, a farmer, of the same place, on the 22nd October. Mr G. C. Chittock appeared for the prosecution and stated that amongst others employed by Mr Gamble was a school boy named Cotterill. On the day in question defendant came into the field where Mr Gamble was and asked why he had been poaching boys from his school. If parents sent their children to school he must let them come. After a few words more defendant hit complainant with his fist and knocked him down, and then hit him when on the ground. Mr Gamble had suffered a lot from the effect of the blows. His eye was blackened, his face cut, and he had also several bruises on his head and back. Evidence was given by prosecutor, Frederick Leatherswick, and Alfred Clarke. Defendant, in defence, said the prosecutor was employing the boy illegally during school hours, and the same thing had occurred three times during the last six months. On one occasion he sent to prosecutor, and asked him to allow the boy to come to school; but no notice was taken of it. He then sent a polite note but prosecutor took no notice of that either. On the day of the assault the lad came to school and had his dinner on the school premises, and Mr Gamble sent for him to go and lead the drill horse in the afternoon. The field where the boy was working was directly opposite the playground, and the other children could see him at work. The magistrates considered it one of the most extraordinary assault cases that ever came under their notice. They could not understand defendant giving way to such a fit of violent temper and committing such an unprovoked assault. He would have to pay a fine of 40s and 12s and 6d costs.

The magistrates' surprise at Higdon's behaviour shows how accepted the custom of employing schoolchildren was. In rural areas, boys were often allowed to do farm work on a half-day basis as long as they attended school for the other half of the day. Regulations for this differed in each locality, but Farmer Gamble may well have been within his rights. Teachers, particularly radical members of the profession like Higdon, had long resented this practice, but farmers claimed that boys would never learn the necessary skills for farm work if they were not taught when young.

The same Mr Gamble became one of the managers of Wood Dalling school in May 1904 – hardly an auspicious event for the Higdons' future. In spite of these setbacks, in a government report of 1904, attendance at the school was reported as being 'excellent' and the Higdons' teaching was praised. Yet in May, the same month that Farmer Gamble joined the Board, the Clerk of the Wood Dalling School Managers wrote to the Education Committee in a confidential report: 'Both Teachers ignore the Managers altogether and are scarcely on speaking terms, with one exception, which is the late Chairman. There is a feeling that a change in both cases is desirable. . . .' The Clerk to the School Managers was also the local Attendance Officer whose job it was to see that the children went to school. He must have been well aware of the good reports of the School Inspectors but had decided to overlook them.

Meanwhile life at the school went on as normal. The Higdons were unusual teachers for their day. They had a gift for arousing the children's interest in subjects outside the normal school curriculum, which consisted mostly of religious instruction and drilling in the three Rs. These were not ignored as one of their pupils' favourite ditties points out:

> Mr Higdon was a very good man
> He tries to teach us all he can,
> Reading, writing and arithmetic,
> But he doesn't forget to give us the stick.

The Higdons also shared their other interests with the children. Kitty would take them on long country rambles. The log book at Wood Dalling records:

27th January, 1903: Mistress took first class for a winter ramble, leaving the school room at 11.15 and returning at 12.40. The ramble was very greatly enjoyed, the children taking keen interest in all the objects seen and discussed and returning to school laden with evergreens, mosses, ferns, stones etc . . .

On clear winter evenings Kitty would take the children out star gazing and, when they had named all the galaxies they could see, they would go back to her cottage for mugs of hot cocoa. Tommy Potter, one of her pupils at Burston, remembered some of her lessons:

> ... she was an extremely efficient teacher. For example we were taught, ... very elementary, but at least we did learn some French, we learnt some Russian, ... she was a very extremely talented organist and she learned [sic] several of the children to play, she also learned them to type, she had a typewriter and she could type and she could teach them to type. She learned, she taught them shorthand. Also we had an Esperanto Class, which I'm quite sure was very unusual for a village school. . . . She taught some of the senior boys to develop photographs, they had a darkroom they called it, I was never one of them but some of them did learn this.

The Higdons also used the school as a place for social gatherings and entertainments. The log book at Wood Dalling records:

> 30th June, 1905: A gramophone entertainment after school was given by Miss Fisher, of Reepham, as an encouragement for good attendance.
>
> 20th December, 1906: The Headmistress arranged for a visit from Father Christmas at 3.30pm and it was a great success, the old gentleman coming in laden with toys, nuts, oranges, sweets, the gifts of Mrs Churchman, Miss Blane (Swiss visitor) and the master and mistress, Mrs Bartram, late Infants Teacher, also sent gift of two shillings which was spent in chocolate for the Infants.

Mrs Higdon managed to organise all these activities, with the help of her husband and a teacher for the Infants, by giving a lot of time to the children out of school hours. She never forgot about the more mundane subjects as this government report shows:

> Plenty of practice has been given in voice training and the singing is sweet. . . . Writing is good and composition is above the average. . . . Drawing is taught practically from natural objects. . . . Knitting is satisfactorily taught.

The children often spent the weekends or evenings at the Higdons' cottage, learning to use the sewing machine, taking part in the domestic chores or just sitting round talking or singing. The Higdons wanted to develop in the children a sense of their own worth and their own dignity. Kitty Higdon stressed the importance of building a life on Christian values, particularly the need to love and care for each other. One of her favourite poems, which she often asked her pupils to recite, was Leigh Hunt's *Abou Ben Adhem*:

> Abou Ben Adhem (may his tribe increase)
> Awoke one night from a deep dream of peace,
> And saw – within the moonlight in his room,
> Making it rich and like a lily in bloom –
> An angel, writing in a book of gold.
> Exceeding peace had made Ben Adhem bold,
> And to the presence in the room he said,
> 'What writest thou?' – The vision raised its head,
> And with a look made of all sweet accord,
> Answered, 'The names of those who love the Lord.'
> 'And is mine one?' said Adhem. 'Nay, not so,'
> Replied the angel. Abou spoke more low,
> But cheerily still, and said, 'I pray thee, then,
> Write me as one that loves his fellow men.'
>
> The angel wrote and vanished. The next night
> It came again with a great wakening light,
> And showed the names whom love of God had blessed,
> And lo! Ben Adhem's name led all the rest.

Although the children were never given a political education in school, the Higdons' socialist views must have had an influence upon them. Mrs Higdon was determined to educate her children, not as fodder for the farm or as slaves for domestic service, but as individuals who could build new futures in a world where opportunities were beginning to open up. The girls were encouraged to develop secretarial skills so that they could leave the village and get work in the towns. For the boys, agricultural labour was still the traditional way of life, but opportunities of work on the railways or as clerks in the local towns provided some alternative.

When he was not busy teaching, Tom was engaged in political activities. He was a leading member of the local Agricultural Labourers' Union, and through his union work he managed to bring about a few small wage increases which infuriated the local farmers, some of whom were Managers of the Wood Dalling Council School. The Chairman of the Managers was a Mr J. J. Bussens, farmer, butcher and landlord of the Jolly Farmers Inn. He was a bluff character who enjoyed chasing young women and had an over-rated idea of his own importance. He was also Chairman of the Parish Council. When Tom Higdon discovered that the Council had been in the habit of handing over the rents from some of the Parish Council cottages to pay local rates instead of spending the money on necessary improvements and repairs, he persuaded the labourers to vote each other on to the Council in the place of the local farmers. Tom was voted in as Chairman, ousting Mr Bussens who was not re-elected. Bussens and the other School Managers were swift to take revenge. Tom Higdon in his own account of the story (in which he has his own shorthand way of referring to himself and Kitty as Mr and Mrs H.) described what happened:

> Suffice it here to say that false complaints against the Head Teacher (Mrs H.) were sent up to the Norfolk Education Committee by the Chairman of the Wood Dalling School Managers and landlord of the 'Jolly Farmers', and that the Committee ultimately decided to remove 'The Head Teacher and her husband' to Burston, where they would be employed by the same County Education Committee, but be under a new set of local School Managers – alas, very much like the old!
>
> Where is there in rural England a body of County Council appointed School Managers who will tolerate Council reforming democrat and Labourers' Union agitator to boot?

The Higdons did not leave Wood Dalling without a fight. They demanded that a representative from the National Union of Teachers should come and put their case at the inquiry set up by the Norfolk Education Committee. Mrs Higdon was accused of calling the Chairman of the Managers and another School Manager 'liars'. Tom Higdon related what took place when the NUT lawyer turned up at the inquiry:

The usual farce of a Local Enquiry, adopted by the Norfolk Education Committee, followed. The NUT lawyer, K.C., arrived a few minutes before the Enquiry commenced, and engaged himself with sending off a telegram about another case. He then spared a few moments to speak with Mrs H. for the first time as to the line of defence to be pursued, which line was to be by way of apology.

'Apologise for a word I never uttered!' indignantly exclaimed Mrs H.

'Whom do you suppose the Committee will believe,' inquired the K.C., 'your Managers or you?'

Mrs H. supposed as the K.C. seemed to suppose.

'Then don't you think you had better admit that you used the word, and I will explain and apologise for you?' was the 'kind' advice of the K.C.

'I did not call the Chairman a liar,' said Mrs H. looking at the lawyer pretty steadily.

'David said "All men are liars",' argued the K.C.

'Then I am glad I am not a man,' said Mrs H., 'and I would not make myself a liar even to make the Committee believe me.'

An Impossible Woman and a Hopeless Case!

For the sake of truth and conscience Mrs H. could not possibly agree with the lawyer mind, however advantageous to herself it might have been to do so.

Apology being the only thing in the mind of the K.C., Mrs H. had brought witnesses to prove that the statements and accusations of the Chairman which she had referred to as 'lies' had been aptly and none too amply described by her as such. The K.C., however, did not call these witnesses, but contented himself with lamely trying to 'smooth matters over', by no means ever hinting that the Chairman had, or could, tell lies. The result was, that the charge against Mrs H. was returned as 'fully proved'.

Chapter 2
Early Days at Burston

Poor and insolvent is the labourer e'er!
Of this the busy Trader must beware
Where'er he brings the labourer's children bread,
Clothes for their backs, or blankets for their bed.

Thus when the Winter's frosty moon is full
They wear their cottons still for want of wool;
And when the chilly rain the byway floods
And the rich stores display their leather goods

With tattered shoes the children trudge to school
Along the lanes' wet slush and muddy pool, –
Preys to diseases springing from their chills
And to the more preventable of ills –
All for the labourer's lack of means to buy
Clothing to keep his children warm and dry!
Tom Higdon, from The Labourer

When the Higdons, bitter about their expulsion and reluctant to take up their new posts, arrived at Burston in the New Year of 1911, they found conditions there to be worse than those at Wood Dalling. Tom Higdon wrote:

> When Mr H. came to Burston, there were no Labourers' Union Branches anywhere in the district, and, consequently, the wages were lower than in the Wood Dalling district. Landlord, parson, and farmer held sway over the Burston area in many respects more completely than in the district left behind. Parson and farmers ruled the Burston Parish Council. Housing conditions were extremely bad, overcrowding occurring seriously. The school premises were ill-lighted, ill-drained, badly heated and wretchedly ventilated. Thus there was much radical wrong, which for very conscience sake, as well as for all practical and healthful reasons, must needs be faced.

Many of the pretty pink-washed cottages that Tom Higdon had noticed when he first entered the village had holes in the roofs and were dark and damp; when families of seven or eight were housed in a small two-up, two-down cottage, the lack of privacy must have been yet another hardship. George Sturt, writing under the name of George Bourne in his journal of a Surrey village, describes the cheek-by-jowl existence of cottage life:

> For it is all such a crowded business – that of living in those cramped dwellings. Besides, the injured and the sick, absorbed in the interest of their ailments, are amiably willing to give others an opportunity of sharing it. The disorder or the disablement is thus almost a family possession. An elderly man, who had offered to show me a terrible ulcer on his leg, smiled at my squeamishness, as if he pitied me, when I declined the privilege. 'Why, the little 'un,' he said, pointing to a four-year-old girl on the floor, 'the little un rolls the bandage for me every evening, because I dresses 'n here before the fire.' That is the way in the labourer's cottage. Even where privacy is attempted for the sufferer's sake there is no refuge for the family from the evidence of suffering. The young people in one room may hardly avoid knowing and hearing where a man is dying, or a woman giving birth to a child, just the other side of a latched deal door.

So must it have been at Burston. A government report* of 1867 states that: 'Burston is an open parish; perhaps ten or twelve owners. The supply of labour is equal to the demand. The supply of cottages is deficient, and many of them are in very bad order, small and over-crowded; the rent much the same as at Dickleburgh.' [The rent at Dickleburgh, a neighbouring village, ranged from £3 to £4 10s a year.]

The state of the school was the Higdons' first concern. Mrs Higdon reported all its shortcomings to the new Rector, the Reverend C. T. Eland, who arrived at Burston shortly after the Higdons. Charles Tucker Eland was a small man whom the villagers remembered as 'ferret-like'. One of them described him as 'a little man with big consequences'. He was called the 'sporting parson' because of his taste for hunting, shooting and fishing. Eland was in his mid-forties by the time he acquired the living at Burston with its large rectory of over twenty rooms and a handsome stipend of £495 a year. He also had 54 acres of glebe land (land owned by the church which was part of the parson's living and could be rented out by him), which produced £86 yearly. He had been promoted late in life and, for the first time, had become a recognised member of the village hierarchy. His wife, who had genteel manners and a passion for large hats, soon made friends with the local farmers' wives whom she could now entertain in style.

Shortly after his arrival, the new Rector was elected on to the Board of School Managers and, as one of his first duties, paid a visit to the school where, according to Tom Higdon, he 'peremptorily demanded the Registers, to inspect them' and soon found cause for complaint against the Higdons. Tom Higdon, as a lay preacher, went round preaching in the local chapels. Kitty had always been to church but, after hearing some of the Rector's sermons, she now decided to go to chapel. Their absence from church did not go unnoticed. According to Tom Higdon:

The parson soon had his grievance – the non-attendance of Mr and Mrs H. at Church. Frequently he reminded them in the

*Employment of Children, Young Persons, and Women in Agriculture (1867) Commission – Evidence.

course of conversation that they ought to go to Church 'for the sake of example'. He often complained to the teachers, too, of the godlessness of the villagers – the inference being that the teachers should set them the example of attendance at Church. He seemed however more inclined to drive the people to Church than to lead them there, and this driving propensity of his they unmistakably resented. He also raised the burial fees; said the Chapel ought to be shut up; likewise said and did many other unpopular things. Mrs H. had been a Churchwoman all her life, and accordingly was in the habit of attending Church when this Rector first came to Burston. She soon felt, however, that she could not profit by his ministrations, and therefore absented herself and went to Chapel – which as mistress of a Council School she had a perfect right to do. 'The place of the school-mistress is at Church and the children with her,' the Rector is reported to have said to one of the parents.

The Rector was not unusual in his attitudes. Most village parsons expected to play a leading role in school affairs. When the 1902 Education Bill was presented to Parliament, a series of articles about the clergy's interference in state education began to appear in the Labour press. 'The new education authorities,' according to the radical journal *Justice*, 'will be whatever the squires and parsons . . . choose to make them.' Another article in the same journal stated: 'The schools have been the happy hunting ground of priest and parson, much more interested in proselytising than in education; the whole administration of elementary education has been in the hands of the classes whose children do not attend our public elementary schools, and amid the din of contending religious factions and the clash of conflicting creeds, the interests of the children have been almost entirely disregarded.'

The families of about half the children at the council school at Burston were Nonconformist and attended the village chapel. In trying to persuade the Higdons to support the church, Eland was playing his part in a long-running battle. As *Justice* comments: 'Between the churches and the chapels the comedy or tragedy of education may be a play with Education left out.'

One of the main aims of the 1902 Education Bill was to replace the old School Boards, run by representatives, elected by local ratepayers, with county borough councils as the local education authorities. The Labour movement fought hard against the abolition of the Boards, which had given local ratepayers some control over their schools. *Justice* states, in October 1902:

> It is true that the establishment of School Boards was a step in the direction of securing direct popular control and the subord-ination of the clerical influences . . .
>
> Instead, however, of perfecting direct popular control, the Government is seeking to abolish it altogether. The education authority in the towns is to be a mainly self-appointed com-mittee, and in the rural districts a committee appointed by the County Council composed of parsons and squires having the least possible interest in the education of the children of the people, except to make them mere humble and obedient wage slaves.

Eland resented Mrs Higdon's attempts to improve the lighting, heating and drainage in the Burston school but, after their experi-ences at Wood Dalling, the Higdons decided to proceed cauti-ously so that there was no open rift between them and the Rector. They were immediately liked and accepted by the rest of the village; a rare thing for outsiders in a small rural place. The villagers were impressed by the Higdons' kindness and genero-sity, and they must have been relieved that their children, after seven rapid changes of teachers, enjoyed the Higdons' lessons. Tom and Kitty were both strict, but they liked giving the children treats. They would buy them sweets for special occasions and every child in the school was sometimes given a bloater when the fish cart came to the village green on Fridays. At Easter all the children were given an Easter egg.

Besides her salary, Kitty had a little private money of her own and she paid for the treats herself and also bought the children clothes and shoes if they were in need. As Tom Potter remembered:

> I've seen her send out and buy children boots, if they came to school and their boots were leaking and this often happened, and she would send out and get them a pair of boots, buy them a pair of boots, I've seen her do it, many times. Also on a

Thursday, once a fortnight, she used to send out and get ginger biscuits . . . and the whole school would have the treat.

Violet Potter, Tom's sister, who was eleven years old when the Higdons first came to Burston, was one of their most loyal supporters. She was a small, dark, lively girl who was always eager to come forward to take part in any activity. As an old lady she still remembered clearly how Mrs Higdon taught them to use a typewriter and sewing machine:

She had an old-fashioned typewriter, probably you wouldn't recognise it today, an old Oliver. And she brought that to School, that was her own, taught some of us bigger children to use that and she had a Singer sewing machine which she also brought to School.

The school day always began with prayers, followed by singing. Kitty played the piano and the children sang. One of her favourite hymns was 'England Arise':

> England arise! the long long night is over,
> Faint in the east behold the dawn appear;
> Out of your evil dream of toil and sorrow –
> Arise, O England, for the day is here;
> > From your fields and hills,
> > Hark! the answer swells –
> Arise, O England, for the day is here!

Tom, whose lesser qualifications entitled him only to act as Kitty's assistant, always sat at the back of the classroom and took the older children. He was a sterner teacher than Kitty. If the children misbehaved he would rap their knuckles with a ruler, whereas Kitty's only punishment was to keep them in after school and give them lines. Teaching two separate groups in the same room could not have been easy. Strict discipline was needed. Most of the children thought Kitty was the better teacher, although they were fond of them both. Violet Potter said of Kitty:

You know you could listen to her and understand what she said different to what you could other teachers . . . a lot of patience she had, especially with the smaller children and yes that's how we got on, we got on well with her.

When the children arrived at the school with wet clothes Kitty would light a fire to dry them. The school's supply of coal was limited and fires were not meant to be lit without the permission of the School Managers. Kitty, determined that the children should not sit shivering in wet clothes, ignored these regulations, much to the fury of the Rector. Violet Potter again:

> . . . . she was very particular with the poor little children, who had a long way to walk to school, they didn't go in buses then you see, and they'd come to school and their clothes would be wet through. So we're not supposed to have a fire until a certain date and she took it upon herself to have fires lit, I think there was a fire at each end of the school, and dry the children's clothes so that they shouldn't have to go home with wet cloaks, and of course that she got wronged for. They was using anything at all to get against her in any way at all they did.

Kitty Higdon hung the children's clothes on the large guards that surrounded the fires so that they would be dry when the children went home at the end of the day. The Managers resented this and accused her of extravagance. They also disapproved of her extra-curricular activities. According to Violet Potter:

> She organised a flower show once in the school playground . . . for the children to bring, you know, what their fathers could send, turnips and things like that and I don't think that they, that wasn't their idea of education. . . . I remember taking bunches of carrots and all sorts of things and we had prizes sometimes and of course the children, when they got a prize . . . went home as happy as could be. I remember I got a prize once for a bunch of carrots. That was one of the things they didn't like about her.

Kitty Higdon enjoyed celebrating the different festivals with the children. On the first day of May she set up a maypole and all the children danced around it. Tom Potter remembered it as one of the high points of the school year:

> . . . always in the middle of the green we'd have a maypole, I mean this was on May Day. . . . May Day was International Labour Day and we celebrated it as a hol, we never had a school holiday, but we celebrated it as a holiday, and on May Day the

girls used to dress the Maypole and I can see them now dancing round the Maypole weaving patterns on the Maypole. . . .

Kitty was well aware that many families could not afford to give their children treats, particularly those children whose parents were ill and could not work, or those from families who had been evicted from their tied cottages because they had lost their jobs. Violet remembered how Mrs Higdon taught them all to make Christmas puddings:

> . . . at Christmas time she thought she wasn't much of a cook herself, but she bought a book to cook by, and she sent out eight, Marjory Ling was one, eight of us into the Schoolhouse to make plum puddings for Christmas and on breaking up day, I think we made about ten of these, she found all the stuff and boiled them in the Council School copper and then the children, they had to bring their own plates and when it was the Christmas holidays they all had this slice of plum pudding each, and that was all out of . . . her own pockets.

Besides making school enjoyable, Kitty wanted to equip the children for the possibility of a better life outside the village and even gave them elocution lessons. Tom Barnes, one of her pupils at Wood Dalling, remembered how they had to practise saying 'Birds build their nests in the Spring.' Yet, in spite of her modern approach to education, Kitty also took a keen interest in country customs and the changing seasons. She once asked the class to write about the coming of spring just as a hailstorm descended on the schoolhouse and the whole class burst out laughing. It is unlikely that the villagers would have accepted her so readily if she had not had a genuine love of the country. Looking back to an earlier tradition, George Bourne, describing his Surrey village, wrote:

> . . . the village people . . . observed the seasons proper for their varied pursuits almost as if they were going through some ritual. . . . And thus the succession of recurring tasks, each one of which seemed to the villager almost characteristic of his own people in their native home, kept constantly alive a feeling that satisfied him and a usage that helped him. The feeling was that he belonged to a set of people rather apart from the rest of the

world – a people necessarily different from others in their manners, and perhaps poorer and ruder than most, but yet fully entitled to respect and consideration. The usage was just the whole series or body of customs to which his own people conformed; or, more exactly, the accepted idea in the village of what ought to be done in any contingency, and of the proper way to do it. In short, it was that unwritten code I spoke of just now – a sort of savoir vivre – which became part of the rural labourer's outlook, and instructed him through his days and years. It was hardly reduced to thoughts in his consciousness, but it always swayed him. And it was consistent with – nay, it implied – many strong virtues: toughness to endure long labour, handiness, frugality, habits of early rising. It was consistent too – that must be admitted – with considerable hardness and 'coarseness' of feeling; a man might be avaricious, loose, dirty, quarrelsome, and not offend much against the essential peasant code. Nor was its influence very good upon his intellectual development. . . . Yet whatever its defects, it had those qualities which I have tried to outline; and where it really flourished it ultimately led to gracefulness of living and love of what is comely and kindly.

Some element of this spirit still survived in the villages of Norfolk just before the First World War and the Higdons, for all their reforming zeal, had a great respect for village life.

Tom wrote a lot of poems about the country and it is interesting that one described a country parson in terms very different from those he would apply to the Rev. Charles Eland:

> His was a dignity of birth and blood.
> He was esteemed of all men everywhere; . . .
> . . . Tho' old his thoughts thro' older channels ran;
> But, in his parish, he was understood;
> And few would dare with him to argue there.
> Your faith at Church was sure to please him well.
> If not a saint, he was a gentleman: . . .

Chapter 3
The Union and the Farmers

A spade! a rake! a hoe!
A pickaxe, or a bill!
A hook to reap, or a scythe to mow,
A flail, or what ye will –
Whatever the tool to ply,
Here is a willing drudge,
With muscle and limb, and woe to him
Who does their pay begrudge!
Thomas Hood

But there can really be no peace or victory for us which does not bring with it freedom for the countryside, liberty and life for the labourer and prosperity and plenty to his home and family. The labourer must henceforth take his place industrially, socially and politically with the best and foremost of the land. He must do this himself – by the force and power of his union. And he can!

Tom Higdon, quoted in The Labourer, *January 1917*

Shortly after Tom arrived at Burston he again became involved in union activities and helped George Edwards to set up a local branch of the ALU which had its origins in an earlier union established by Joseph Arch. Arch was the son of a Warwickshire labourer. Like Tom Higdon, he was a Primitive Methodist and a lay preacher. He learnt to read and write at the village school but was mostly self-educated. As he wrote in his autobiography:

> I was wonderfully fond of my books and my writing. I did not want to go into the street and play with the other boys; I stayed indoors and stuck to my self-set lessons. My mother would set me copies, give me writing tasks and sums to work out. She was always ready to help me, willing to explain a difficulty, or smooth out a knotty point if she could. She was as anxious that I should get on as I was myself.

He became a skilled labourer and, having mastered the arts of hedge-cutting and mowing, he travelled around the countryside:

> The Midlands and South Wales was my beat and I kept my eyes and ears wide open, while going on my hedge-cutting and mowing rounds. I saw that there was a smouldering discontent among the different classes of agricultural labourers with whom I was brought into contact, but they did not make any effort to improve their position. I would ask the men who worked under me whether they were satisfied with their condition, and their answers were almost without exception in the decided negative.

Wherever he worked, Arch spread the idea of forming a union, but it was not until 1872 when 'things were going from bad to worse with the bulk of the labourers in our neighbourhood' that the time came which he had long waited for.

> It was a very wet morning and I was busy at home on a carpentering job; I was making a box. My wife came in to see me and said, 'Joe, here's three men come to see you. What for, I don't know.' But I knew fast enough. In walked the three; they turned out to be labourers from over Wellesbourne way. I stopped work, and we had a talk. They said they had come to ask me to hold a meeting at Wellesbourne that evening. They wanted to get the men together and start a union directly. I told them that, if they did form a Union, they would have to fight hard for it, and they

would have to suffer a great deal; both they and their families. They said the labourers were prepared both to fight and to suffer. Things could not be worse; wages were so low, and provisions were so dear, that nothing but downright starvation lay before them unless the farmers could be made to raise their wages. Asking was of no use; it was nothing but waste of breath, so they must join together and strike, and hold out till the employers gave in. When I saw that the men were in dead earnest, and had counted the cost and were determined to stand shoulder to shoulder till they could squeeze a living wage out of their employers, and that they were the spokesmen of others likeminded with themselves, I said I would address the meeting that evening at seven o'clock.

Arch found himself addressing a meeting of nearly 2000. The news had passed by word of mouth, and labourers had come from within a ten-mile radius. A resolution was passed to form a union immediately and plans were made for another meeting in a fort-night's time. At the second meeting the labourers planned to strike for an increase in wages to sixteen shillings a week (the average wage was about twelve shillings at this time). News of the strike and of the newly formed union soon spread to neighbouring counties and branches began to spring up in Oxfordshire, Herefordshire, Leicestershire, Somerset, Norfolk, Northamp-tonshire and Essex. Arch saw his dream of a national agricultural labourers' union becoming a reality.

On 31 March 1872, the *Eastern Weekly Press* carried a leader on the strike by the Warwickshire farm workers. The *Press* was a radical paper which circulated throughout Norfolk and aimed 'to guide the working classes politically and morally'. There had been a drop in the agricultural workers' wages in the years before 1872 and there was much discontent. Union meetings were soon being held all over the county but many of the Norfolk unions, unlike those elsewhere, were keen to keep the leadership of the union in the hands of local people and to concern themselves with local issues. The unions split into two factions: some were pro-Arch and wanted to be part of a national body but others supported local leaders who wished to make their unions independent. By the 1880s, as the agricultural depression worsened and the labourers realised that they were not able to bargain for higher wages, support for the unions dropped off considerably and by the early 1890s the Norfolk unions had collapsed altogether.

One of the early union leaders who began as a member of Arch's union and later became strongly opposed to centralisation was George Edwards. He was a brick maker who had taught himself to read when, as a Primitive Methodist, he became a lay preacher. As he wrote in his autobiography:

> Up to this point I could not read, I merely knew my letters, but I set myself to work. My dear wife came to my rescue and undertook to teach me to read. For the purpose of this first service she helped me to commit three hymns to memory and also the first chapters of the Gospel according to St. John . . . when I returned home from work after tea she would get the hymn book, read the lines and I would repeat them after her.

The Bible was also the inspiration for his political ambitions:

> With my study of theology, I soon began to realise that the social conditions of the people were not as God intended they should be. . . . Many a time did I vow I would do something to better the conditions of my class.

When the first union movement collapsed in 1896 Edwards retired. 'I was,' he wrote later, 'a disappointed man, having lost all faith that my class would be manly enough to emancipate themselves.'

In the early 1900s changes began to take place which provided new hope for the labourer at a time when he seemed utterly defeated. By 1902 wages had improved, harvest earnings were high and there was a constant supply of work. Arch's early unions had helped to develop in the farm workers a more independent attitude and new aspirations. As a Dorset clergyman wrote: '. . . the Revolt of the Labourer began under Arch. And by revolt I mean the expression by every means in his power of his independence of the classes to whom he had hitherto been in submission.' The 1906 landslide victory for the Liberals put new heart into the Union's cause. Every Norfolk seat returned a Liberal and, in the two-member Norwich constituency, the traditional balance of one Liberal and one Conservative was upset when a typographer, G. H. Roberts of the recently created Independent Labour Party was voted in, one of 29 successful Labour candidates throughout the country. Although Roberts was not a country man and had had little to do with village life he soon became the labourers' spokesman. His election gave a great spur to the Norfolk Labour movement and there followed a period of feverish political activity throughout the county. Both the Liberals and the Socialists began to campaign for the labourers' rights and these campaigns helped to give the farm workers a new sense of their own worth. When Edwards (whom one labourer described as 'a little humpety-backed man') bi-cycled round Norfolk, he discovered that many men were keen to build a second union. This second union was less chapel-orientated than the first. Quite a number of Methodists had grown rich in the intervening years and were keen to forget their radical past. Edwards found he was no longer welcome in many chapels as a lay preacher because of his 'radical social sermons'. Union meetings were seldom held in the chapels; more often in the local pub. The older leaders, like Edwards, were less mili-tant. He had seen too much misery caused by the unsuccessful strikes of the 1890s and, by the time Tom Higdon arrived on the scene, much of Edwards' former fighting spirit was lost.

Although Tom was at first resolved to proceed cautiously at Burston, because of his recent experiences at Wood Dalling, he had soon taken up his old custom of riding round the countryside on his bicycle, getting to know all the local labourers. He also held meetings in the pubs and pointed out the benefits of forming a union. Winifred Potter later remembered accompanying Tom on some of his trips to union meetings. She came to realise how closely interlinked were his love of the country and his political ideals:

I was a keen cyclist . . . and he used to ask me to accompany him and I used to ask him if I could, you see it was a mutual thing, and the cycling journey was very enjoyable and of course the meetings equally so, but I remember the pleasure of cycling with Tom, and on one night in particular. That was when we had a meeting at Thetford which was some 20 miles from Burston and, cycling back, Tom got off his bicycle and asked me to do the same to listen to the nightingale sing in a wood and it was really beautiful because it was wooded country and it was a still night and it was really enchanting to hear these nightingales; and this was one aspect of Tom's character, that he loved the nature of the country, nature in itself and this I think inspired him quite a lot with his work, in his efforts to raise the standard of life of the people who lived in such surroundings.

Tom was a persuasive speaker, and it did not take long to get the men round to his way of thinking. He listened carefully to their problems and heard about the poor conditions of the old footpaths, the dilapidated houses and crumbling bridges which the Parish Council had failed to repair. Tom decided to use his old tactics to take over the Parish Council at Burston.

As at Wood Dalling, the Parish Council consisted almost entirely of local farmers. The land around Burston was mostly let to tenant farmers. After the long agricultural depression of 1875–95, land values had rapidly decreased. The cheap imports from the colonies and shipments of American wheat had put many farmers out of business. Those who ran large estates with sufficient capital to invest in the land, or smallholders who ran their smallholdings on family labour, were sometimes able to make a profit but the worst hit were the small-time farmers who needed to employ extra labour, for at least part of the year, to work their land. Many of the farmers around Burston were in this class (although some tenant farmers had as little as thirty to fifty acres).

Rider Haggard, the popular Victorian author, lived on the other side of Norfolk. A few years earlier he had written about small-time farmers of the Burston kind:*

> . . . there is a third class of farmer – the 200 or 300 acre man – impregnated with the traditions of fifty years ago. Often he thinks it beneath his dignity to work in the field alongside of his labourers, and finds it necessary, even though he has nothing to sell or to buy, to attend a market at least once a week. For that man, I think, the future holds no good in store. He is apparently doomed to disappear.

*In *Rural England – Being an Account of Agricultural and Social Researches carried out in the years 1901 and 1902*, volume II (Longmans, Green, and Co., 1906).

On the east coast of Norfolk, Rider Haggard met one of the largest farmers in the neighbourhood, Mr Beck, whose farms had halved in value since 1875. (He noted that one of Mr Beck's farms which had cost him £70 an acre was now not worth more than £35.) As land was no longer profitable and since it was subject to tithes and taxes which had to be paid regardless of profit, many of the larger landowners were selling off their land. Rider Haggard met a farming friend of Mr Beck's who had sold off his land for this reason:

Mr. Wiseman, a resident in the neighbourhood, who I saw at Mr. Beck's, said that he used to farm 1,000 acres, but then had only 250, which he would give up were it not for the value and comfort of his house. He did not believe that one farmer in ten was actually solvent. Mr. Wiseman gave me some figures, taken from the accounts of his home-farm of 170 acres in the years 1878 and 1900, which show so clearly how great is the fall in the value of the produce from a given acreage of land in this locality that I print them.

1878

Cr.		Dr.	
Stock and crops £1,245		Rent £450	
		Labour £290	
		Bills	
		etc. (about) £200	
			£940
Profit £305			

1900

Stock and crops £668		Rent £205	
		Labour £320	
		Bills etc.	
		(which are higher in proportion than in 1878 about £200	
Loss £57			£725

35

Mr. Wiseman added that his profit on each bullock used to be from £8 to £10, but during the previous three years it had not averaged £5 a head, although they had eaten an acre of roots apiece in addition to cake. He said that of labour they had sufficient, but owing to the pace at which the men worked it took ten horses to do what used to be done with eight. The young men, he added, were not going on to the land, from which their parents discouraged them. He could not see where any improvement was to come from or how prices were to be heightened. The only man who had a chance was he who worked his holding with the help of his family, and of doing this people were apt to get tired.

American wheat imports were one of the worst threats to arable farmers (Burston was a corn-growing area). As Rider Haggard recounts:

Mr. Wade considered the outlook very uncertain. It was, he said, difficult to see much light when a sack of wheat could be delivered from America for less than it cost to send it from Watton to London.

The soil around Burston is a rich, heavy clay which produces a high yield of wheat per acre, so farming conditions were less serious in this area than in other parts of the county but bad harvests could still wipe out any chance of a farmer at least breaking even on his investment.

Another problem for the tenant farmer was security of tenure. Farmers on short leases could find themselves threatened with eviction and the land being sold over their heads. One farmer reported in 1912:

No doubt you are well aware that one of the chief drawbacks to successful farming is the lack of security in tenure. Unlike any other industry, a farmer to succeed must look at least two or three years ahead; under our present system of tenure this is impossible, as at the most he can only count upon 12 months' occupation.

I am not in a position to give the cause, but never in the

memory of any man have so many farms been placed on the market as there has been during the past six months; these changes in many instances inflicting great hardships upon the occupying tenants. . . . The farm I now occupy, and the two adjoining ones, are for sale. These are offered in one lot and not separately to the tenants. I may say that I have been six years tenant. When I entered the farm was in a derelict condition, and for twelve months had been tenantless; the 'away' going crops belonging to my predecessor of so-called corn were one mass of docks and thistles – the height of myself. During the six years I have spent a considerable amount in cleaning the land, cutting and laying hedges, cleaning out every pond and ditch on the farm etc.

Should these farms change owners, in all probability I should have to leave next April, as mine is a six months' agreement and for the above improvements I cannot claim one penny as compensation, the owner getting the benefit.

The main landowner in the area who rented out nearly all the farms to the Burston tenant farmers was Sir Edward Mann of Mann's breweries. He lived several miles away at Thelveton and had sufficient capital from his family business not to be dependent upon his land. He showed little interest in his farms and never interfered in Burston affairs so the local tenant farmers were more secure than most, but the problems facing their fellow farmers must have added to their own sense of insecurity.

Only one man on the Parish Council, Noah Sandy – a smallholder and bricklayer – was independent of the farmers. It was Noah who first came to the school to ask Tom if he would like to be nominated for the Council.

Mr H.'s thoughts immediately flew back to the Wood Dalling Parish Council Election when, with the aid of the labourers there, he routed the farmers and set up a Labourers' Parish Council. He related the event to Noah, and told him how the new Council soon stopped the farmers' game of handing over to the district rate the rents of some Parish cottage property, and instead spent it on necessary improvements and long overdue repairs for the benefit and comfort of the tenants. Noah – otherwise 'Noar' – blinked his heavy-browed eyes knowingly.

A rare type of old rustic Radical was 'Noar'. He soon tumbled involuntarily to the new Labour idea and, what is more, showed a ready willingness to give the whole revolutionary plan a trial at Burston – a willingness to advance in Progressive thought and action which has characterised the Burston labourers throughout the long and hard struggle which was then about to begin.

Higdon was once more enthusiastically engaged in what he described as 'Parish Council democratic reform'. He started at once to get a sufficient number of labourers nominated, along with Noah and himself, to fill the Council. He knew this campaign would almost certainly bring about the same disastrous results for him and Kitty as it had at Wood Dalling but, by this time, after two years of seeing their efforts at Burston thwarted by the parson and the farmers, his blood was up.

Chapter 4
The Parish Council Elections

We plow and sow, we're so very very low,
That we delve in the dirty clay;
Till we bless the plain with the golden grain,
And the vale with the fragrant hay.
Our place we know, we're so very very low,
'Tis down at the landlord's feet:
We're not too low the grain to grow,
But too low the bread to eat.

Ernest Jones

The Parish Council elections were held in March 1913. Tom Higdon described the meeting:

At the Annual Parish Meeting the Council Schoolroom was packed – much to the surprise, apparently, of the old Council of farmers, who sat ceremoniously at the front, waiting for their re-election, or rather awaiting the moment to re-appoint themselves – the parson being amongst them as a new candidate in the sure and certain hope of his own preferment to a seat on the Council.

The names of the candidates were read out alphabetically, those of the 'Cabinet', so to speak, as represented by B. E. F. J. thus happening to come before the letters of the Labour men, such as the P's, the W's and the S. Of the Labour Party, H. only came before J.

On the platform surprise took the form of consternation when it was observed that most of the earlier candidates failed to reach two figures. Surprise and consternation were plunged into the silent rage of anger and despair when the figures leapt up to their zenith at H. and down again almost to zero at J; J being the initial letter of the Chairman of the old Council, a leading farmer and a Churchwarden. The P's, the W's and the S came close up behind H. It was clear the game was up for the 'Government'. F., the letter representing a local farmer who used not to be considered a bad sort, just managed to come in at the tail end of the list of elected members. The fact of this solitary farmer's election was not altogether to be regretted, as it supplied the new 'Government' with an 'Opposition' sufficient to swear by. F. swears too, occasionally, very audibly, typical Churchwarden as he is, and as he is very hard of hearing, his solitary presence on the 'Opposition side of the House' has at times produced a good deal of loud shouting from the new 'Ministerial Benches'.

Tom Higdon came top of the poll with thirty-one votes and the Rector came bottom with only nine. According to Tom's account, the Rev. Charles Tucker Eland's attitude towards him showed a marked change after the Parish Council elections. The Rector did not attack Tom directly but he began an active campaign against Kitty Higdon as the Headmistress of the school. As the posts of

Headmistress and Assistant Master were joint appointments, the dismissal of the one automatically included the dismissal of the other.

Eland took up his old grievance of the Higdons' non-attendance at church and, one Sunday, he decided to take Mrs Higdon to task for it. Tom wrote:

> Upon the present occasion, Mr and Mrs H. had been taking a refreshing Sunday morning walk and enjoying a quiet afternoon read when the Rector, fresh from the Creed, the Ten Commandments and the Churchwarden's dribble, paid this second after-service visit to the Schoolhouse. Why on Sunday after Church? Why not on a week day? He talked long and pertinently upon the importance of Church-going. . . . The Rector evidently very much desired to say something more – much more – but seemed unable 'to get it all out,' and finally went away, leaving a rather uncomfortable impression behind him as to what was the real nature and meaning of his visit. Mr H. did not say much at this interview, but Mrs H. fully discussed with him the merits and demerits of Church-going. Very unwise of her, no doubt!

A few weeks after the Parish Council elections, it became necessary for the Norfolk Education Committee to appoint a new Board of School Managers for Burston Council School and Eland saw his chance. The Norfolk Education Committee was authorised to nominate five members, the sixth being the nominee of the Parish Council. The Committee consulted the local J.P., Mr Keppel, and he, in turn, consulted Eland who suggested himself, his wife, his friend, the Rector of Shimpling, the latter's Churchwarden and his own glebe tenant. The Parish Council's nominee was Mr Witherley, a farm labourer. All these were duly elected and Eland was appointed Chairman. He had brought off a successful counter-coup – all but one of the School Managers were his loyal supporters. As Tom Higdon wrote: —

> Mr. Keppel, J.P., C.C., of Scole, is responsible for the recommendation to the Norfolk Education Committee of this ecclesiastic clique. Mr. Keppel seems to have been as easily 'got at' or 'got over' as Mr. Wade, of Shimpling [former Chairman of

the School Managers], was 'got out'. Will Mr. Keppel say how he came by these nominations? Two parsons and a parson's wife on a body of six Council School Managers!

Leaving the affairs of the school in the hands of his new School Managers, Eland left for a holiday in Switzerland. A local journalist who called himself 'Casey' wrote an account of the events that took place at Burston and described what happened then:

> The Reverend Charles Tucker Eland, to give him his full title, departed this Burston village life for a short holiday in Switzerland.
>
> A clergyman's holiday has two good points. It gives both him and his congregation a well-earned rest. Whilst the Reverend School Manager was away in Switzerland, an epidemic of whooping cough had the audacity to enter the village.
>
> Mrs Higdon, the schoolmistress, at once sent over to another reverend school manager, the Reverend Millard (Rector of Shimpling and vice-chairman of the local Managers' Committee), and he, after consultation, decided to close the Council School for one week. He signed the notices, and made an entry in the log to that effect.
>
> When the Rector of Burston arrived back from Mount Pilatus another meeting of the school managers was held.
>
> This Managers' Committee informed Mrs Higdon, through the chairman (Reverend C.T. Eland this time) 'that the committee took a very serious view of her having closed the school without permission, but,' added the Reverend Pulpiteer, no doubt in an outburst of holiday extravagance, 'the managers will now let the matter drop.'

Eland may have thought that Mrs Higdon's prompt action to stop the epidemic made him look foolish in front of his fellow managers. Whatever his reasons, he let matters rest until November when he discovered that Kitty was again lighting fires without permission. Without discussing the matter with her, on 29 November, he wrote to the Norfolk Education Committee complaining that she had acted against the School Managers' instructions and that 'as she had so many faults to find with the place, would the Committee kindly remove her to a sphere more genial?'

When they received Eland's letter, the Education Committee decided not to act immediately on his recommendations. The building inspector's report showed that the school was damp and that it was necessary to make a number of alterations before the drainage system could be described as satisfactory. Instead they took the safer alternative of sending Mr Ikin, Assistant-Secretary to the Norfolk Education Committee, to give Mrs Higdon an official warning. Casey described what happened:

> The next act opens with the appearance of Mr Ikin, Assistant Secretary to the Norfolk Education Committee. He paid what is known as a surprise visit.
>
> A surprise visit is the most modern form of torture. . . .
>
> His surprise words to Mrs Higdon were: 'What is wrong between you and the Managers?'
>
> Mrs Higdon replied that she was not aware that there was anything wrong.
>
> Mr Ikin went on to say that the local managers had written to the Norfolk Education Committee, complaining that she had lighted the schoolroom fire against their instructions, and that 'as she had so many faults to find with the place, would the Committee kindly remove her to a sphere more genial?'

The Norfolk Education Committee followed up this visit with a letter in which they stated:

> I may remind you that this is the second place in which you have come into conflict with the managers.
>
> The Committee have decided that the managers' instructions are to be obeyed, and as they have instructed you that the fire is not to be lit, I am to give you directions to obey these instructions. I trust there will be no further friction.

It was signed: Thos. A. Cox, Secretary.

Casey commented:

> . . . The schoolroom fire was lit upon wet mornings to dry the children's clothes as the third radiator of the heating apparatus did not sufficiently warm the room. The Reverend Eland visited the school and the mistress explained to him her reasons for lighting this fire occasionally. Strange to say, he agreed with

her, and advised her to write to Mr Wade, of Shimpling. He not replying (according to his usual practice), silence was taken as consent.

Not before a new body of managers was formed, with the reverend gentleman, who had previously given his permission, as Chairman (C. T. Eland), was the complaint re fire resurrected.

Eland must have realised that his complaints about fire-lighting were too slight to bring about Mrs Higdon's dismissal. He soon had some more serious charges to put before the Committee.

At the school there were two Barnardo's children, Ethel Cummings and Gertie Stearness, who were being fostered by Mrs Philpot, a woman who was not popular in the village. She was known to be mean and slatternly and had a bad temper. She received a certain sum of money from Barnardo's each week for the upkeep of the children and this was paid out to her by the Rector, who was the Barnardo's local representative. Mrs Philpot claimed that her girls had witnessed one boy's 'rude' behaviour (he was said to have exposed himself in the school playground). Gertie Stearness had only arrived at the school the day before the complaint was made. Violet Potter gave her version of the story:

> . . . one of the girls' names was Ethel Cummings, they were two Dr Barnardo's children, I suppose they had no parents and this person, Philpot her name was, adopted them. Well she had to do that through the Rector, you see, and . . . I think she was a bit afraid of him really. I know where she lived in Burston, the house isn't the same now but still, I know exactly where and he went to see her and told those children, drilled into those children to say that Mrs Higdon ill-treated them. Well they said so, and that was a complaint . . . and it was all untrue because Marjorie and I and Hetty we, she said you elder girls, you . . . talk to these children when in the playground and see what they've got to say, and the children themselves told us they were told to say it, that it didn't happen at all. . . . And of course the poor little children were afraid otherwise because I don't think she was a very good foster-mother. Anyhow I think she was very

very strict . . . and they did as she told them and the Rector put her up to this and of course she was afraid of losing the children, losing the money because she got so much money for them and he would take them away if she didn't. . . .

Mrs Philpot also stated that Mrs Higdon had beaten the girls with a cane and that they had been sent home with weals on their back. This was a surprising charge to bring against a schoolmistress who was known to be a pacifist and averse to all forms of violence. Tom Higdon recounted what happened next:

> Mr H. reminded Rev. E. that the little girl who had made the complaint about rude conduct had only been admitted to the School one day before these tales were started by her. Mr H. also told the Rector that upon the girl being questioned she had said it was in the School she had come from where she had seen these things.
> . . . He also gave proof from the Registers that the boy complained of was not present at School when the rude conduct was said to have taken place; while all the school children and teachers knew quite well that the Mistress had not punished the girls at all, but that she had only questioned and admonished them upon their false stories about the boy. She had in fact sent for the boy's mother, who came to School and saw and heard her boy completely vindicated by the girls themselves, who turned upon one another, each accusing the other of hatching the story. . . .
> The girls themselves, when questioned at School, freely confessed that the boy had not been rude to them and that they had not been beaten by the Mistress. They said they were told to tell these stories and that they were afraid their 'mother' would beat them if they did not. All the assembled School heard this confession of the Barnardo children. They also made this confession to the infants' teacher, Mrs Ling, when speaking to her alone. But neither the Rector nor any representative of the Education Committee or of Barnardo's would ever come to the School to hear it.

The Higdons wrote several letters to Dr Barnardo's to recommend that the children should be removed from Mrs Philpot's care. In one of these letters, they stated that Ethel Cummings was mentally and morally defective and a danger to the school. According to Casey, the Barnardo's girls were living in 'one-storied insanitary hovels, with outside walls only seven feet high, and damp rooms on the ground floor, unfit for sleeping in'. The Barnardo's Homes did not send a representative down to inspect these living conditions or investigate the charges made against Mrs Philpot. Instead they merely sent Mrs Higdon's letter on to the Rector, who triumphantly wrote off to the Education Committee. His letter, dated 23 January 1914, states that:

On December 10th, Mrs Philpot, the foster-mother of two little girls, aged eight and nine respectively, from Dr Barnardo's Homes, had occasion to write the Mistress in reference to the rude behaviour of some boys in the School and the indecent conduct of one in the playground. These charges the Mistress denied and accused the little girls of lying and being corrupters of the School. The Managers met and requested the presence of the Mistress but she did not appear. They interviewed Mrs Philpot and the little girls and were satisfied that they spoke the truth, so instructed the Clerk to write the Mistress to that effect and that the children were to return to the School after the holidays and were to be treated as the other children, and also that should there be any further complaints they would be reported to your Committee. Notwithstanding these instructions, on the re-opening of the School on the 5th inst., the Mistress brought out these girls before the whole School, cross-questioned them and kept them in during playtime, day after day, with the object of making them contradict themselves, wrote letters and telegram to Barnardo's Homes concerning them and Mrs Philpot with the view of having the children removed.

The Managers have gone into these charges and find they are without any foundation. Under all these circumstances the Managers feel at loss what to do and ask the Committee to hold an investigation and they consider this constant haranguing the whole School on this unpleasant subject, most tactless and detrimental to its tone and discipline.

Owing to the insubordination and rudeness of the Mistress,

there is no esprit de corps between her and the Managers and they find it impossible to work with her, so respectfully ask she may be transferred.

It is interesting that the Rector never referred to the caning incident in his letter. He also did not mention that Mrs Higdon was ill when the Managers' inquiries were taking place. According to Tom Higdon:

A clear day prior to one of these Managers' 'Enquiries', at which it was found in Mrs H's absence – she being absent under doctor's certificate – that there was 'good ground' for the complaints of the Barnardo foster-mother, Rev. E. called at the School and, failing to see Mrs H., saw Mr H., to whom, with much mock gravity he related the Barnardo foster-mother's story about what he alleged to be the rude conduct of a boy towards two Barnardos' girls in the playground, and what he described as Mrs H's ill-treatment of these Barnardo girls by severely caning them.

Mr H. emphatically denied the whole story, the rude conduct allegation having already been investigated by Mrs H., and assured the Rector that if he would visit the School in the morning, he would find that there was not a word of truth in the complaints. The Rev. Chairman, however, seemed wilfully and perversely adamant. He did not say he would come. He did not come. Why did he not come? Mrs H. sent a special request to him and still he did not come. She also sent to the Rector of Shimpling and he did not come. Evidently they wanted 'Enquiries' – but no real enquiry.

Chapter 5
Official Inquiry – and Dismissal

Of the poor's poverty the causes moot
The Parson scarcely cares to know the root;
He fain would not disturb the bare or green
Of things that are – and for long time have been!

Rejoicing in his own by ancient right
He bids the poor be thankful for their mite, –
Happy himself, Christ's minister, to serve,
Shoot o'er his sacred glebe and his preserve, –
To dine off beef or game, or fish in Lent,
And take his honoured toll of tithe and rent!

Tom Higdon, from The Labourer

The Higdons also wanted an inquiry and consulted the National Union of Teachers, but the union wanted to avoid making it an official issue and sent down one of their representatives, Mr Peggram, to persuade the Higdons to come to terms with their employers. However, Tom and Kitty stood their ground. Tom wrote:

> Mr Peggram, whom the NUT sent down from London to talk matters over with Mr and Mrs H., after calling out 'Keep smiling on the Managers', as his train was moving off from the Burston platform, returned to London, and sent back Mrs H. a letter, which she was to send to the Education Committee assuring the Committee that she had not punished the Barnardo girls 'excessively'.
>
> She had not punished them at all, and had assured Mr Peggram so; she therefore, of course, refused to send this letter. She simply could not send such a letter and thus diplomatically admit herself in the wrong, contrary to the facts, in order that she might be forgiven for what she had never done. This kind of thing may do for the NUT; it would not do for Mrs H. This was Wood Dalling over again. No, no, Mr Peggram! Yet some hopes, after all, were raised that the NUT did intend to fight.

The NUT, having previously had to defend the Higdons at Wood Dalling, had no doubt branded them as troublemakers. It reluctantly agreed to provide legal assistance with the warning that: 'Under these circumstances you must of course accept full responsibility for the results of any such inquiry.' The Norfolk Education Committee sent down three councillors to hold the tribunal: Mr Sancroft Holmes, Chairman of the NCC, a landowner and farmer, and a former Tory Parliamentary candidate for Burston; Mr Jessup, a Tory farmer; and Mr Goldsmith, a Liberal farmer. They all lived in the Burston district and knew of Tom's work for the Agricultural Labourers' Union and of his attempts to improve housing conditions in the village against strong opposition from the local farmers. The charges against Kitty were: 1) discourtesy to the Managers; 2) punishment of two Barnardo's children; 3) writing letters of complaint against the foster-mother to the Barnardo's institution; 4) insubordination, rudeness, and lack of 'esprit de corps' shown by the headmistress towards the

Managers. The inquiry lasted two days during the last week of February 1914. Kitty Higdon was ill and did not put in an appearance but she was represented by Mr H. Lynn, the NUT standing counsel. According to Tom Higdon, the first day passed off well:

> Two afternoons were given to the Enquiry, a Monday afternoon and a Friday afternoon in the same week. Mr Cooper (NUT Lawyer's Clerk) visited Burston, and went round the parish collecting evidence. Mr Cooper was delighted with the signed statements he obtained and seemed confident of victory for Mrs H. 'A beautiful case! A beautiful case!' he exclaimed.
>
> Mr K.C., too, at Monday afternoon's hearing, showed some spirit, and did not do at all badly. The Sub-Committee then found that the alleged 'Discourtesy' was 'very slight', but that a 'very serious view' was taken of the caning of the Barnardo children . . .
>
> Mr K.C., however, easily cleared Mrs H. of the 'Fire-Lighting Contrary to Instruction' charge and of the 'Rude Conduct' allegation, and apparently established the view that the alleged 'Discourtesy to Managers' was very slight. Had he not asked for an adjournment of the Enquiry but finished the job off that afternoon, he might have scored other goals. But the President of the Enquiry, Mr Sancroft Holmes, it seems, could not remain, so the adjournment asked for by Mr K.C. was granted.

The Rector, seeing that the case was not going well for him, called in a Norwich solicitor, Mr Reeves, to act for the School Managers. On the following Friday, when the tribunal considered the allegations of Mrs Philpot, the NUT Counsel, in Tom Higdon's view, badly mishandled the case:

> Mr K.C. put up no fight at all that afternoon. He attempted no cross-examination whatever, but allowed many most important points and false statements to pass unnoticed and unchallenged. Indeed, it seemed as if Lawyer Reeves was, by mutual consent, to be allowed to have things all his own way. The Barnardo children were thus put through their 'pieces' again in the most seductive manner possible. Brother Farmer Fisher smiling and nodding and bending and bowing towards them all

the while, especially when the 'drilled lies' were being repeated. This was evidently manna to his soul! Did not the K.C. of the NUT know what a farce he was permitting?

'Why did the Mistress cane you?' said the President to one of these Barnardo girls.

No answer. (Puzzled)

'Was it for saying the boy was rude to you?' thus putting the words into the child's mouth.

'Yes, Sir.' (Happy Deliverance)

Yet it was not found that the boy had been rude to these children and the point had been dismissed. . . .

This and much more of vital consequence to the case Mr K.C. let pass – which, together with the aforesaid apparent intentional omission of evidence, considerably gave the case away. Still, for all that, had the Sub-Committee had eyes that wished to see they could well have seen. They did see. The NUT saw. It was an agreed thing that the teachers were to be dismissed.

The Rector's two witnesses were called. Tom Higdon describes them as:

. . . two old women, one of whom was the mother of several illegitimate children – seven they say. The other was the Churchwarden's washerwoman who had felt herself bound to attend the Enquiry when told to do so. . . .

The former dear old dame came to say she had seen rude conduct in the playground by some infant boys. Rude conduct, indeed, Madam! What about your own?

The other crone had a fairly easy time of it in hypocritically white-washing the Barnardo foster-mother, whom she had formerly been in the habit of painting black.

Mrs Philpot, who had begun to lose heart after the first day's hearing, is said to have come out of the second and final day of the inquiry shouting, 'I'm not dead yet! I'm not dead yet!'

As the Higdons expected, the case went against them. Casey, the local journalist who spent a lot of time in the village in the months following the Higdons' dismissal, wrote in his account:

That two respectable teachers should be hounded out of house and home simply upon the testimony of a poor Barnardo waif – who privately denied what she publicly confessed, excusing herself by saying 'she would have been thrashed by her foster-mother if she had not said so' – seems beyond belief.

Still the fact remains that Mrs Higdon did not cane the child, as the whole of the school children can prove. She does not belong to the cane family. Furthermore, the sequel to this complaint proves her entire innocence. Pity, indeed, is it that those who were seeking excuses for her removal could not find a single parent or child belonging to the village to complain of Mrs Higdon's treatment of them.

Casey then cited the Enquiry Report which led to the Higdons' dismissal:

● That the head teacher has been discourteous to the Managers.

● That in view of the direct conflict of evidence with respect to the caning of the Barnardo children they are not able to give a decision on this matter; but they are strongly of the opinion that there is no evidence at all that the girl (E.C.) is mentally and morally deficient or a danger to the school, as stated in the letters of the head teacher and her husband. (The head teacher said she was 'somewhat' mentally deficient, which, of course, alters the context.)

● That, in their opinion, these children are well treated and cared for by their foster-mother, and that the children are not afraid of being beaten by her.

● That in their opinion the communications sent by the head teacher and her husband to Dr Barnardo's Institution were not warranted by the facts of the case.

The sub-committee, after most carefully reviewing the whole of the evidence, advise: 'That it is to the interest of elementary education in this village that the head teacher should seek other employment with as little delay as possible. That no punishment book having been kept in this school by the head teacher prior to this occurrence, she be directed faithfully to keep such a book.'

So the forces of reaction had triumphed. . . .

The inquiry was practically a funless farce. Higdon and his wife received short notice to vacate the School (left in the lurch by the NUT, as at Wood Dalling and at Burston, where the representative, after promising that a slander action would take place as soon as possible, became frightened at his own bravery, and thought better of it), they felt inclined to understudy poor Joe, and move on.

The Higdons were told by the NUT Counsel that their witnesses had not been called at the inquiry because they were being kept for the slander case; after the inquiry, as Casey states, the promise of a slander action against the School Managers was quickly forgotten. Tom Higdon tried to take up a slander action privately but was advised that it would cost a lot of money so, reluctantly, he let the matter drop.

Mrs Higdon's alleged acts of discourtesy to the Managers were again, as at Wood Dalling, the prime reason for her dismissal. These 'acts' of Mrs Higdon's included failing to acknowledge the Rector when he and his daughter cycled past her; failing to notice the Rector when she was buying some vegetables from an itinerant greengrocer outside the school; not giving enough attention to the Rector's wife when she visited the school in her capacity as Manager and, when called to a Managers' meeting, she was accused of entering the room without knocking and sitting down without greeting any of the Managers.

A few days after the Committee had written to Mrs Higdon asking her to 'seek other employment', the Higdons received two days' notice to leave the school, by 31 March. Tom Higdon wrote that:

Mr Ikin, Assistant Secretary, appeared at Burston Schoolhouse early on Wednesday morning, April 1st, with cheques for salary in lieu of notice – which, on being refused by Mr and Mrs H. were left by Mr Ikin upon the Schoolhouse table.

Not only had the Education Committee been interfering in the Higdons' affairs: while Tom and Kitty prepared for their last day in the school, there was a general outcry in the village as parents and children heard about the Higdons' dismissal. The children were busy with secret plans of their own. With the backing of their parents, Violet Potter and a group of the older children were making arrangements to go on strike. They planned to stay away from the school rather than accept the new teachers brought in by the Education Committee. Violet decided to make a list of all the children who were willing to join them.

> I said to them 'We want to know who's going out on strike and who isn't?' Well all but about six said that they would come, I think it was about 72 children went to School then and I put the names down on a sheet of paper that I'd got all ready and that night, when Mr and Mrs Higdon finished up, we stayed behind and helped to – Marjorie [Ling] and I did – and helped to . . . take her possessions indoors because she'd got her sewing machine and her camera and her typewriter and a lot of personal belongings in the School . . . and we took them into the schoolhouse. We slipped back into the School. I turned the blackboard up, we . . . had a blackboard and chalk and I put 'we're going on strike tomorrow' and turned it to the wall so that the teachers that came the next day, the new teachers, when they came to use this blackboard that's what they would see.

Kitty Higdon knew nothing of these activities, which stemmed from a meeting of the parents and children that had taken place on Burston Green on the evening of 31 March. The meeting was chaired by George Durbidge who had a fish stall and was a well-known figure in Burston. He was a large man, over six foot tall, who could be charming and kind when in a good temper, but was also subject to fits of violence, being a heavy drinker who frequently got himself involved in pub brawls. All the village and even the local constables were afraid of him but, surprisingly, he was a loyal supporter of the Higdons. He was the father of six children, one of whom, Sabina Durbidge, was a friend of Violet Potter's at the school, and obviously felt himself to be a natural leader of the other parents who no doubt would not have dared to think otherwise. Under Durbidge's direction, the parents and children had gathered around his fish stall, lit by large flare lamps, on the village green. A report in the *Norwich Mercury* describes what took place:

Tuesday evening, on the green. The Common was illuminated by two large flare lamps, lent by Mr G. W. Durbidge, who presided over the meeting. . . .

The Chairman proposed the following resolution: 'That we, the people and ratepayers of Burston, and the parents of the children attending Burston School, do most emphatically protest against the high-handed action of the Education Authorities in terminating the services of Mr and Mrs Higdon at the Burston School. Under the unjust circumstances, we protest against the introduction of new teachers to the School, and we urgently request the County Education Authorities to reconsider the whole matter with a view to our retention of the teachers whose services are so generally appreciated amongst us. That owing to the mischievous interference with the conduct of the School in regard to the Barnardo children, we protest against their attendance at the School, and their presence in the Parish.' The resolution, having been seconded by Mr Noah Sandy, was put to the meeting and carried amidst deafening cheers.

Sol Sandy, a young man at the time, remembered the meeting well in later years:

It was getting dark, we had these flares, and at the meeting they sent a resolution, I believe, to the House of Commons, and he [Durbidge] told them to. . . . 'Stick, stick, stick, like bloody shit to a blanket!'

George Durbidge's closing words to that crowd of parents and villagers were not forgotten. They did stick together against all the odds. Besides being a fish-hawker and a well-known poacher, Durbidge was also, according to Tom Higdon, an avowed Conservative but that did not alter his sense of loyalty to the Higdons. Almost the whole village, except for those who were connected with the church or under the influence of the local farmers, came out in a body to show their support. They publicly cheered the Higdons and let out groans and hoots for the Rector. It was the first time they had got together as a group and outwardly challenged the status quo. It must have been an exhilarating experience.

Not all the men of the village were agricultural workers. Some of the luckier ones worked on the railway (Burston was on a direct line to London) and were already benefiting from the improved pay and working conditions brought about by the National Union of Railway Workers, one of the most powerful unions in the country at that time. The railwaymen were independent of the local farmers, more secure in their jobs, and better off in all respects than the agricultural labourers. Those who lived in or near Burston took a keen interest in the Higdons' cause and were well aware that Mrs Higdon was being victimised because of her husband's work for the Agricultural Labourers' Union. George Bourne's description of the artisans in his Surrey village shows how new prospects of work could open up the outlook of the whole community:

> And just as, amongst the skilled craftsmen, there are individuals representing every stage of the advance from five-and-twenty years ago until now, so the earlier stages at least of the same advance are represented, one beyond another, by labouring men in this village. I could not find any labourers who are so far forward as the forwardest artisans; but I could find some who have travelled, say, half the way, and many who have reached different points between that and the stagnation which was the starting point for all. Hence I cannot doubt that the villagers in general are moving on the route along which town artisans have passed a generation ahead of them. They are hindered by great poverty; hampered by the excessive fatigues of their daily work; entrammelled by remnants of the peasant traditions which still cling about them; but the movement has begun. The first stupefying effects of their eviction from the peasant life is passing away, and they are setting their faces towards the future, to find a new way of life. . . .

By the time the meeting was over on Burston Green it was agreed by all those present that the schoolchildren should go on strike the following day, the day the Higdons were due to leave the school, and both parents and children hurried back to their homes to make preparations.

Chapter 6
'We Want our Teachers Back'

To the tune of 'Heart of Oak'

Come gather, O People, for soon is the hour
When Princes must fall with their pomp and their power;
For the power of the Future, we know it shall be
A People united and soon to be free

Chorus

Firm and fast we will stand
Heart to heart, hand in hand
In rain or foul weather;
Brothers together –
A people united and sworn to be free

E. Nesbit

None of those involved could remember whose idea it was to go on strike but such action was not uncommon. A wave of school strikes in 1889 and again in 1911 had aroused a good deal of public interest. Stephen Humphries in *Hooligans or Rebels* states that:

> The 1889 school strikes originated in Hawick, Roxburgh, at the beginning of October and rapidly spread throughout the Scottish lowlands, the Tyneside area, as far south as London, Bristol and Cardiff. The 1911 strike began at Bigyn School, Llanelli, on 5th September, when pupils deserted their classrooms and paraded the streets after a boy was punished for passing around a piece of paper urging his friends to strike. During the following two weeks the strike spread to schools in over sixty major towns and cities throughout Britain. . . .
>
> The rapid diffusion of strikes in both 1889 and 1911 was viewed by most commentators as a consequence of the conformity, gullibility and unlimited capacity for blind imitation of working-class children and youth. This claim was substantiated by the fact that most major school strikes tended to occur at times and places at which parents were engaged in either local or national strike action and by the sensational publicity given to the children's activities by the popular press. Thus, the editor of the *Educational News* in 1911, for example, confidently assured his readers that 'The cause . . . is easy to find. Men tired of work. . . . strike. "Striking" conversations are meanwhile carried on in their homes to the detriment of all else. Naturally, children are possessed of powers of . . . imitation, waiting only to be called into play. . . . Hence "strikes", being the fashion with adults, become likewise that of the juveniles. The daily press has done much to spread the epidemic; for instead of paying little heed to the pranks of the scholars in one or two towns, has published full details . . . and a real game of "Follow the Leader" has been the result.'
>
> However, oral evidence indicates a more subversive explanation for school strikes, one that is related to deep-rooted class conflict. The characteristic features of both these major strikes – notably their nationwide scale, the widespread use of pupil pickets and street marches and demonstrations – were all derived from the practices of the emerging labour movement.

Certainly this was the fear of the *Dundee Advertiser*:

> It has not yet been ascertained through what medium schoolboys received the signal for united action. . . . Such movements as this do not spring up spontaneously. They are always evidence of a deep conspiracy against social order. . . . It is perfectly evident that the schoolboys from Land's End to John o' Groats could not without organisation arrange to strike simultaneously. The doom of the Empire must be near at hand if the country is honeycombed . . . with Secret Societies of schoolchildren. . . .

Editorials on school strikes in the *Educational News* of October and November 1889 portray them as a form of social disruption which can easily be remedied: 'The rod is the sure cure for strikes.' One such claimed that:

> Schoolboy strikers . . . are simply rebels. Obedience is the first rule of school life. . . . School strikes are therefore not merely acts of disobedience, but a reversal of the primary purpose of schools. They are on a par with a strike in the army or navy. . . . They are manifestations of a serious deterioration in the moral fibre of the rising generation.

Although many school strikes collapsed after a few days and failed to achieve their aims, they did help to bring attention to conditions in the schools. Pupils aged ten went out on strike in protest against severe canings; in the 1911 strikes children argued that the older pupils who were being used as monitors in understaffed schools should be paid a small weekly sum and, in 1889, London schoolboys in Kennington and Lambeth went out on strike demanding free education; one free meal a day; no home lessons; no punishment (by caning).

Stephen Humphries again:

> Another way in which pupils and parents sought to assert community control over provided education was through strikes to support the retention of teachers whose position was threatened by local authority interference or to press for the dismissal of unpopular or incompetent teachers. The most prolonged and powerful strike action brought by pupils occurred in Herefordshire in 1914, when children supported the

county's National Union of Teachers members' militant demands for salary increases. The children's resistance began at the beginning of February, when, in response to the union's strategy of mass resignations, the local education authority appointed new teachers, many of them unqualified, to replace those involved in the dispute. Pupils in towns and villages throughout the country expressed sympathy for their former teachers, who were among the lowest paid in the country, by refusing to be taught by the new members of staff, and seventy schools were forced to close. The most violent scenes occurred at Ledbury Girls' School, where a riot developed in which desks were overturned, and the new headmistress was chased off the premises by a crowd of girls chanting 'Blackleg'.

It is interesting that this strike happened in the same year as the one at Burston. The following year, Emily Wilby, a pupil at Burston School, wrote an account of 'Our School Strike' which was published by Lusher Bros. of Diss:

We came on strike on April 1st., 1914. We came on strike because our Governess and Master were dismissed from the Council School unjustly. The parson got two Barnardo children to say that our Governess had caned them and slapped their faces, but we all know she did not. Then our Governess lit a fire one wet morning to dry some of our clothes without asking the Parson. So the head one said that our Governess and Master had better be got rid of. They had their pay sent and two days' notice to leave the School. Governess did not know we were going on strike. She bought us all some Easter eggs and oranges the last day we were at the Council School.

Violet Potter brought a paper to School with all our names on it, and all who were going on strike had to put a cross against their name. Out of seventy-two children sixty-six came out on strike.

The first morning our mothers sent the infants because they thought they did not matter, but in the afternoon they too stopped away and only six answered the bell.

The next morning the sixty-six children lined up on the Crossways. We all had cards round our necks and paper trimmings. We marched past the Council School and round the

'Candlestick' [a local name for a route round the village]. When we got to the foster-mother's house, she came out with a dustpan and brush to 'tin' us, but when she saw our mothers she ran in. She put a card in her window with 'Victory' on it, but she has not got it yet. Some of our parents gave us cake and drink and many other things. When we got to the Crown Common we had a rest. Mrs Boulton, the lady at the Post Office, gave us some lemonade and sweets and nuts. She also gave us a large banner and several flags. At twelve o'clock we went home for dinner. At one we marched again. When we got up to one of the foster-mother's friends . . . she jumped up from behind a hedge and began to 'tin' us. When we hooted her she said she would summons us, but it has not happened yet. . . .

As this account makes clear, the strike at Burston was a disciplined, well-organised one. The strikers followed a pre-arranged route round the village; the children and strike supporters had prepared their banners the night before. Violet Potter and some of her friends made sure that all the children were there and formed them into a procession. She brought along an accordion and some of the other children had mouth organs which they played in accompaniment to the strikers' song, 'Heart of Oak':

> Come, cheer up, my lads, 'tis to glory we steer,
> The prize more than all to an Englishman dear;
> 'Tis to honour we call you, not press you like slaves –
> For who are so free as the sons of the waves?

At the school gates the strikers passed a disapproving audience which included Mr Ikin, two of the School Managers, the two new supply teachers, and the Police Inspector of Diss but the procession went on its way, undaunted, as Violet Potter remembered:

. . . one was a police sergeant stood by and one or two of the church wardens, they'd evidently got an inkling that something was going to happen, and of course we went by and singing and that and Mr Durbidge leading us and, never took any notice, didn't even look, went marching right round The Candlestick and came back out on to Crown Green. . . .

Before they reached the small patch of green before the Crown

Inn, where refreshments were waiting for them, the children marched up to the Rectory and booed the Rector. Mr Eland had kept well clear of the proceedings which he mistakenly dismissed as an April Fool's jest and a 'nine days' wonder'.

In fact, the event was already making some stir beyond Norfolk. Besides reports in the local press, two London national newspapers ran stories on the strike. According to the *Daily News and Leader* of 3 April 1914:

> The children of the Council School of Burston and Shimpling, Norfolk, have gone on strike as a protest against the dismissal of the Headmistress, Mrs Higdon, and her husband, who was also on the School staff.
>
> Yesterday only seven scholars met the two imported teachers. The other children paraded the district carrying a banner inscribed 'We Want Our Teachers Back'.
>
> The dispute originated in complaints made by the School Managers, of whom the Rev. C. T. Eland, Rector of Burston, is Chairman, that Mrs Higdon had ill-treated children from Dr Barnardo's Homes. The mistress and her husband totally denied the allegation, and asked for an inquiry. The County Committee investigated the matter with the result that Mr and Mrs Higdon were called upon to resign.
>
> The sympathy of the inhabitants is strongly with the deposed teachers, and the opinion is freely expressed that political motives underlie the matter, Mr Higdon's views on politics being opposed to those of the Rector and the majority of the Managers.
>
> Public meetings have protested by large majorities against the dismissals and resolutions have been passed declaring that Mr and Mrs Higdon have been unfairly treated.

The *Daily Chronicle* of 24 April 1914 also suggested that the Higdons had been dismissed for political reasons:

> The parents demand an official explanation from the Norfolk Education Committee of the dismissal of Mrs Higdon, the head mistress, and her husband, the assistant master, and they insist also on a public inquiry to clear up a mystery surrounding the causes of the Committee's action.

Both Mr and Mrs Higdon are supporters of the Agricultural Labourers' Union, and Mr Higdon is an official. 'I am a labourers' man – that's the top and bottom of it,' he declared yesterday. . . .

After the procession the children continued to stay away from the school and the new teachers. This challenge could not be over-looked by the authorities, and within a few days the Norfolk Education Committee had summonsed eighteen of the parents for failing to send their children to school, in compliance with the Education Act. Emily Wilby described what followed:

One day a policeman went round to twenty houses with summonses because we had not been to school. The day we were to appear at Court all the big children dressed up and went to the Crossways. We started for Court about half-past-nine. As we were going along we sang our old Strike Song. Before we started we had oranges and chocolate.

When we got down to Diss several people were lined up each side of the street. We left our parents at the Court and we went into the Park. Mrs Robert Wilby brought us some refresh-ments, ginger beer, etc. Some of the girls went to the Court to see what the time was. There a man took their photos. The fine was half-a-crown each. When our mothers came out of Court we went into the Market Place and had some bread and cheese and some ginger beer. Governess bought us some cakes to eat on the way home. Mrs Boulton gave us some chocolate. Then we started for home. When we got half-way home we sat down and had a rest and ate our cakes. We got home about six o'clock.

The strike had by now become an important local event. News of the Burston protest had spread to London and other parts of the country and the local press were devoting a great many column inches to the affair, giving lively, detailed accounts of the Court cases. The *Diss Express, and Norfolk and Suffolk Journal* reported on 24 April 1914 that:

Considerable interest and excitement prevailed on Wednesday when eighteen parents whose children's names are on the list of scholars at Burston and Shimpling School, appeared before the magistrates at Diss Petty Sessions for neglecting to send their children to school. The occasion was taken advantage of to make a demonstration of the youthful strikers, who adorned with various colours, carrying banners and flags, and wearing cards bearing the words 'We want our teachers back', 'We want Justice', etc . . . marched from Burston to Diss. They sang some of their favourite school songs as they covered the distance of three miles separating the two places. The roadway outside the Court was thronged when the children, who were accompanied by a number of parents and friends, arrived. At first they were led into the 'Two Brewers' yard but the police interfered and would not allow them to remain on licensed premises. As other cases had to be disposed of, the defendants, the strikers and their friends had to remain for some time outside the Court, the limited accommodation of which was severely taxed. . . .

The list of defendants included John Aldrich, labourer; John Bridges, signalman; Joseph Cobb, labourer; George Durbidge, fish dealer; Joseph Ford, labourer; Walter Garnham, labourer; Henry Gotts, labourer; Edward Huggins, platelayer; Harry Ling, shoemaker. The charges against them consisted of unlawful neglect in not sending their children to school at Burston on 7 April. The information was laid by the Attendance Officer at the instance of the Norfolk Education Committee. Mr H. G. Davis, of Norwich, appeared for the prosecution.

The first case taken was that of John Aldrich. Upon his appearance Mr Davis asked that all the other defendants should be admitted to the Court as the remarks he had to make to the Bench would apply to each case. The names of the other defendants were then called and they or their representatives came into Court.

Mr Davis, addressing the Bench, said this and all the other cases had arisen from what was called the Burston School Strike. The engagement of the head mistress and assistant-master at Burston School terminated on March 31st, but he did not intend to go into the reasons of it. Firstly, it did not affect the case, and secondly, he did not know what the reasons were. It was only fair to say that the public through the Press had only heard one side of the case, because a public authority could not

A portrait of Tom Higdon as a young man taken at East Pennard in Somerset (probably by his brother, Frank, who was a professional photographer)

Kitty Higdon, probably taken around the time of her marriage

A formal portrait of Tom Higdon

Mrs Higdon at the First Anniversary celebrations (top left); *Tom Higdon talking to a striker at the door of the carpenter's shop, 1 April 1915* (top right); *Young strikers at the First Anniversary celebrations, 1 April 1915* (below)

The procession, First Anniversary celebrations (above)*; Mr and Mrs Higdon, the striking children, parents, and friends, on Burston Green, 1 April 1914*

Violet Potter, aged 13, when she was the children's strike leader

Mr Harry Ling and his soldier son, standing on the glebe land of which the family had to give up possession. The land had been held by the Lings for about a hundred years

Mr and Mrs Garnham at Burston in 1916 (above); *Some of the Burston Strike supporters (with Tom Higdon, in a trilby, in the back row). The picture, probably taken by Mrs Higdon, still hangs in the Burston Strike School*

The upstairs room of the Strike School. From left to right; Marjory Ling, Elsie Mullinger, Hetty Wilby, unknown, Jack Mulligen and Reg Potter (above); The carpenter's shop, drawn by one of the Durbridges

The cottage the Higdons moved into after their eviction from the Schoolhouse and temporary accommodation at the Mill. At first they lived in the right-hand cottage, and later they also bought the adjoining one (above); *A group of determined Burston mothers who supported the strike. From left to right: (top row) Mrs Harry Ling, Mrs Durbridge, Mrs William Wilby, Mrs Wells; (bottom row) Mrs Bob Wilby, Mrs Thirza Moore (known as the Warrior Queen), Mrs Potter (mother of Violet and Tom)*

Some of the first pupils at the Strike School (above); *Pupils posing with Tom and Kitty Higdon in front of the entrance to the Strike School. (Tom Higdon is in the far left-hand corner and Kitty is in the centre)*

Tom Higdon in 1916

Tom and Kitty Higdon in the late 1930s, shortly before Tom's death

Tom Higdon's funeral in 1939 (above); *Commemoration stone on the Strike School*

Interior of the Strike School 1985 (above); *Former pupils posing outside the Strike School in June 1985. From left to right: Win Potter, Barny Ford, Stella Lantsbury, Ron Leeder, May Moore (nee Wilby), Arthur Moore, Tom Potter, Frank Bloomfield*

Eileen Atkins as Kitty Higdon in a scene from the BBC TV film

enter into a newspaper controversy. They had heard that the dismissal of the head mistress and her husband was the result of a private inquiry. It was true a private inquiry was held, but Mr and Mrs Higdon had the benefit at that inquiry of a solicitor and a barrister acting on their behalf. Under these circumstances their case must have been brought forward properly. It was greatly to the credit of Mrs Higdon and her husband that they had endeared themselves to the parents and the children. But that, he contended, had nothing to do with the case. Since the dismissal of Mr and Mrs Higdon, none of the children of the defendant had attended the school. If they had any excuse he would meet it, but he could not understand that they had any. Therefore he asked the Bench to deal with the cases seriously, and show the defendants that they could not flout an established authority. . . .

The Attendance Officer having given formal evidence the defendant said he should not send his children to the school. He declared that the two children from Dr Barnardo's Homes had caused all the trouble, and they wished for them to leave before their own children returned. They wanted a public inquiry.

The Court was cleared while the Bench considered the matter. They came out in favour of the Education Committee although they were clearly not unaware of the strong local feeling in support of the Higdons:

The Magistrates felt they were bound to support the prosecution ordered by the Education Committee, and at the same time they felt bound to acknowledge the fact that there was a very strong feeling in Burston of affection and regard for the mistress and assistant master, and the parents were no doubt distressed at the idea of parting with the old teachers. The Bench were willing to make allowance for that because it was not altogether an unnatural feeling. But the Education Committee who had the management of the School wanted it conducted in the most efficient way. Therefore they felt it did not become individuals or individual parishes to deal with a case like this in the way Burston has done. . . .

The Magistrates decided they should go along with the prosecution, but give the parents only a light penalty. They were all
fined 2s 6d, although some of the parents put up a spirited
defence, as the *Diss Express* records:

The next case was that of John Bridges who admitted that his
child was not at school and said he did not agree with the
decision of the Education Committee. He should like a public
enquiry to ascertain the truth.

The Chairman told him he believed he had power to invoke
the aid of the Board of Education in the matter of a public
enquiry. He would be fined 2/6.

Joseph Cobb pleaded not guilty and asked for a public
enquiry.

The Chairman said: The penalty will be the same.

George Catchpole was represented by his wife who admitted
that her daughter Elsie was not at school on April 7th. She
would be fined 2/6.

George Durbidge said he could not say if his son Frank was
at school or not.

Mr Starr produced a certificate that the boy was absent on
the date mentioned. Defendant: How many times were Dr
Barnardo's children absent? – I cannot say. – Did you go to Dr
Barnardo's children? – No. – Will you tell us how many times
they have been absent? – No; it has nothing to do with this case.
– Why are you not instructed to deal with Dr Barnardo's
children? – I cannot say. – Defendant said he had not sent his
son because he thought the late teachers had been unfairly
treated. Parents who had to clothe and keep their children and
pay for their education had an absolute right to know who was in
fault and who was not. They were all satisfied with the education and the treatment their children were receiving, and it
was only right and proper that the parish should know why the
teachers were dismissed. All they asked for was justice. If there
was a public enquiry and the parents were in the wrong, the
children would be sent to school. He had written to London to
the NUT and he had received an answer that his letter would
have attention. The Education Committee would not hold a
public enquiry because they did not want the reasons put before

the public. Until the teachers were proved to be wrong the parishioners would have to take their own course.

Defendant was fined 2/6 ...

Edward Huggins was quite willing to send his son to school but asked for a public enquiry. – The Chairman: We cannot order a public enquiry, we can only deal with this case; fined 2/6.

Harry Ling said his daughter Marjorie went off to school at the usual time, and when she got there she joined the strikers. What was he to do? Was he to force the child into school against her will?

Mr Bryant: What would you do if there was anything else you did not want her to do?

Defendant said he had a conscientious objection to the child going to school. She would sit all alone and fret and pine for the head teacher.

The Chairman: That is not sufficient reason for dealing with yours differently to the others. He was fined 2/6.

Alfred Moore admitted his son was not at school and was fined 2/6.

Thomas Mullinger also admitted that his son Jack was not at school.

The Chairman: Any reason to give?

Defendant: No, only he was on strike and he dare not break the rules. (Laughter)

The Chairman: We must not break the rule. You will be fined 2/6. (Laughter)

John Potter, sen., was represented by Mrs Potter, who said she should not send her son unless there was a public enquiry, because she thought there had been injustice done. She did not see why they should be ruled by a parson. (Cheers)

Clerk: That has nothing to do with the Bench. – He was fined 2/6 ...

The hearing over, the return journey to Burston was made into a triumphant demonstration by the strikers, and sufficient money was collected from well-wishers to pay for all the fines.

At the close of the Magisterial enquiry, the children formed up outside the Corn Hall, where a big crowd collected. To the strains of 'Hearts of Oak' a march was made through the town, and on returning to the Market Place, the little ones were kindly provided with refreshments. The children were accompanied by a number of parents, some of whom carried collecting boxes in aid, it is said, of the 'Fine' Fund, and they evidently met with many sympathisers among those who were interested in watching the proceedings.

The parents were summonsed again, as Emily Wilby recalled:

Our mothers were soon summoned again. This time the children did not go. They went a little way, then they came back. This time the fine was five shillings. There were thirty-two of our parents summoned. Our parents did not have to pay a penny of the fine, it was all collected on the Green and in the streets. At night we went to Diss to meet our parents. When we got there we had some ginger beer. A man took our photos for the living pictures. Then we went to see them; they were very good. Mr Sullings gave us a free performance.

Chapter 7
The School on the Green

Bread and Roses

As we come marching, marching, in the beauty of the day
A million darkened kitchens, a thousand mill lofts grey
Are touched with all the radiance that a sudden sun discloses
For the people hear us singing, 'Bread and Roses, Bread and
  Roses.'

As we come marching, marching, unnumbered women dead
Go crying thro' our singing, their ancient song of bread.
Small art, and love, and beauty, their drudging spirits knew:
Yes, 'tis bread we fight for, but we fight for roses, too.

As we come marching, marching, we bring the greater days,
The rising of the women means the rising of the race.
No more the drudge and idler, ten that toil where one reposes
But a sharing of life's glories, 'Bread and Roses, Bread and
  Roses.'

James Oppenheim

By now, in response to the parents' request that Tom and Kitty should carry on teaching their children, lessons were being held regularly on the Green. Luckily it was a dry and sunny April. As Emily Wilby recalled:

> We had school on the Common a little while, then we went into the very cottage that the Barnardo children had lived in for a year and a half. Our mothers lent stools, tables, chairs, etc. . . . Mr Ambrose Sandy said we could have his shop for a Strike School. Sam Sandy came and whitewashed it out and mended the windows. He put a ladder up so that we could go upstairs. . . .

The Higdons kept a register and followed a proper timetable.

> *9 am* School opened with a hymn and prayers with Mr and Mrs Higdon.
>
> *10.15 am* Playtime. [A short break]
>
> *12.00 pm* Break for dinner. [Most of the children went home. Some stayed and ate sandwiches with Mrs Higdon who always had a cheese sandwich and water in a medicine bottle.]
>
> *1.30 pm* Afternoon school. [This often included games on the Green, usually football or cricket. In winter they went sliding on the pond and in May they danced round the maypole.]
>
> *4.00 pm* School ended. [The younger children were often taken home by the older ones and Mrs Higdon would take home the children who lived near her.]

Lessons were mainly given by Mrs Higdon. Tom was often present in the schoolroom doing Union business. The Education Committee may have felt that there was some justice in the parents' claim that they were sending their children to the school of their choice. In any event, no further summonses were issued against them for the children's non-attendance at school.

The Committee's next step was to evict the Higdons from the schoolhouse (their cottage was attached to the school building, and occupancy went with the job). Tom Higdon gives a lively account of what took place:

> Then came a warning of eviction from the Committee, followed by the Eviction Notice, and finally by eviction itself. Mr W. E.

Keefe, of Norwich, argued in vain before the Diss Magistrates that the payment of salary in lieu of notice did not discharge the obligation to allow the usual three months' notice for vacating the Schoolhouse. He afterwards stated in 'The Labourer' that had funds been forthcoming he would like to have appealed against the decision of the Diss Bench.

Mr Cox, the Committee's Secretary, on oath, declared before the Bench that Mrs H. was given three months' notice. He caused quite a sensation in Court by so doing. How Mr Cox reconciles this to his Conscience it is hard to tell. Salary in lieu of notice cannot by any stretch of imagination be held to cover a three months' tenancy of a cottage. Yet such the Norfolk Education Committee! Such the Diss Bench of Magistrates.

Men, women, girls and boys, miller's cart, donkey cart, wheelbarrows, all without fee – joined joyously and sympathetically in the enforced removal of the dismissed and evicted teachers' goods – to coalholes, to larders lacking their proper furniture, to village stores and divers other places wherever storage room could be found.

Thus, what might have been a sorrowful and trying day was turned into a glad and happy one by such loving gratuitous and self-sacrificing service. It was such a tiring day, nevertheless, yet, at night, when Mr and Mrs H. finally went back to the Schoolhouse, to lock up before going to their proffered lodgings at the Mill, they found a large number of villagers gathered on the bit of moonlit lawn – mothers, fathers, girls, boys, babies, bless them! When were they not there? Only when duty bound them elsewhere; and there they remained until midnight. . . .

After the Higdons left the council school premises, all the strikers' meetings took place on the Green or in Ambrose Sandy's carpenter's shop. Every Sunday large public gatherings took place on the Green. The chapel congregation had swelled to such large numbers (the Rector's church congregation having dwindled to only a small group of his personal supporters) that Methodist services, baptisms and even funerals were conducted on the Green. The services, led by Mr John Sutton, who had been a lay speaker at Burston chapel, were followed by Strike meetings. As the weeks went on, these became a regular rallying point for sympathisers from as far as Norwich and beyond. A local newspaper provides a report of a typical Sunday meeting which was attended by members of the Independent Labour Party:

> Owing to showery weather the usual outdoor meetings in connection with the school strike did not take place on Burston Common on Sunday afternoon, but the 'Strike School' – a disused carpenter's shop – was packed with parents and parishioners. A party of nine members of the Norwich Branch of the Independent Labour Party cycled over and two, Mr R. J. Ingram, a member of the Norwich Town Council, and Mr Aylmer Richardson, took part in the proceedings, which were conducted by Mr John Sutton, of Burston, who read the lesson and offered a prayer. Mr Ingram said he was present to convey the sympathy of the Independent Labour Party with Mr and Mrs Higdon. As to the issue of the fight the parents were bound to succeed if they stuck to one another and to the dismissed teachers. A collection was taken in aid of the Parents' Defence Fund.

The Green became the centre point for all the important events in the village. Several 'Strike' funerals took place on the Green; one of the most tragic of these being that of George Durbidge's daughter Sabina, who died suddenly of meningitis. Emily Wilby gives a detailed account of the Rector's and the farmers' interference in her burial – behaviour which suggests that by now their response to events was becoming irrational and hysterical.

> We have had three strike funerals. The first was that of a little boy who got burnt to death. Mr Williams buried him. When the little boy's father paid the sexton for digging the grave, the sexton asked for the parson's fee. The father was full of grief; he paid the parson his fee. The next funeral was that of a little girl who died very suddenly. There was an inquest. A jury of farmers and Parson's men was called together and they tried to make out the child died because she came to the Strike School. They asked the poor mother what time the Strike School fire was lighted, and didn't the children go to meet Governess and

Master without any hats, and didn't they have to go across a Common with water on. They called the poor mother into the room three times to worry her with questions. At the inquest the doctor told them why the girl had died. They would not believe him and ordered a post-mortem which is the cruellest thing there was. After that the doctor told them the same thing he did at first. The way they treated the poor mother was brutal. After the funeral Governess told the poor mother to come into school and she made her a cup of tea and told Mr Durbidge that the poor mother should not be teased by those men any more. So he went and told the jurymen that his wife was not well. . . .

Meningitis often results in unexpected and sudden death and Sabina Durbidge, having complained at school in the morning that she was not feeling well, was taken home and died later the same day. The farmers tried to turn Sabina's death into a public scandal by implying that conditions at the Strike School were the cause. As Tom Higdon wrote:

Yet another dastardly attempt to wreck the Strike School was made by a mean and spiteful endeavour to fasten the death of a little girl upon her attendance at the Strike School, notwith-standing the doctor's evidence to the contrary. The child had died of meningitis. An adjournment was demanded by the farmers present at the inquest, and a post-mortem examination was ordered, much to the pain and mortification of the parents. The plot utterly failed, and brought nothing but contempt upon the authors of it. . . .

Having dropped any more attempts to summons the parents for their children's non-attendance at the Council School, there was no further interference from the Education Committee. A new pattern of life began to emerge for the whole village. The children attended classes regularly either on the Green or in the old carpenter's shop. As Reg Groves writes in *Sharpen the Sickle*:

In fine weather the Higdons held classes on the Green. But a building was needed for wet or cold days, and for this purpose they rented the workshop of an old blind carpenter [sic] named Sandy. Villagers gave chairs, tables, stools, lamps, mats and even pictures for the walls: the women washed and scrubbed and scoured; the men whitewashed and painted. The Strike School, as it soon became, was visited by County Councillors, by inspectors, by school attendance officers and others: they could find nothing wrong. Indeed, the children were keeping up regular attendances in all weathers, and all were happy under their teachers. The Higdons were now unpaid teachers, and to remedy this the villagers clubbed together to raise small sums of money, and brought gifts in kind to the schoolhouse, gifts of eggs, fruit, butter, jams, vegetables and milk. The National Union of Teachers helped by paying the Higdons' victimisation pay. [This change of heart came later.]

Meanwhile, news of the Burston meetings was spreading through the press and the Labour Party journals, and they grew and grew. Leading lights from the Labour movement in London and their followers would come down by train to Burston to attend the Sunday meetings. Burston became used to seeing such radical luminaries as George Lansbury, Philip Snowden, Bruce Glasier, John Scurr, Tom Mann and many others. They would arrive by train from London and be greeted by the villagers who would march with them in a triumphant procession to the Green. Reg Groves writes:

> On Sunday, July 15, 1914, a big meeting was held in Burston. No less than eighteen trade union banners were ranged around the Green; a brass band came from Norwich, and a special train from London brought down another brass band and hundreds of railwaymen, who had taken the cause of Burston to their hearts. There were speeches, the children sang songs and did country dances, 'Casey' brought his fiddle. . . .

The London visitors often stayed the night with the villagers. Arthur Moore, one of the Burston pupils, remembered one of these weekend visits:

> Well, that particular meeting that I remember is that we had nine train load from London one Sunday and we had a big marquee up on the Crown meadow . . . and that was for people to get in and we had to organise . . . food and drink for 'em. In fact a lot of 'em come from Norwich and about and they stopped the night, came on Saturday and stopped the night and some of

'em you know were put up for the night and . . . any person could take home about half a dozen and give 'em tea.

The meetings and the services on the Green were all reported in the local newspapers. On Saturday 20 June 1914, the *Diss, Harleston, Bungay, Beccles and Eye Journal* records:

Last Sunday was 'children's day' in connection with the open-air services that are held on the Green. There was a good attendance at each service, which was conducted by Mr John Sutton afternoon and evening. The singing of special hymns and recitations, given by several of the children and others, were attentively listened to by the onlookers, who much enjoyed the efforts of the performers. The singing was accompanied on the organ by Mrs Higdon. Recitations were said by Violet Potter, Hettie Wilby, Emily Wilby. . . . Solos were sung by Mlle. Houze (in French) and Alice Turner. A trio was sung by Violet Potter, Marjory Ling, and Lilian Bridges, and a hymn by Joe Ford, Jack Mullinger, Bob Wells, Willie Wilby, Reggie Gotts, Fred Durbidge and Bertie Huggins.

The collections which amounted to £1.19s.6d. will be devoted to a tea to be given to the children.

While these outdoor activities were in full swing, questions about Burston were being asked in the House of Commons, as the same journal reports:

Mr George Roberts asked the President of the Board of Education if he had received a petition signed by the parents of the children who had been withdrawn from attendance at the school at Burston, and a majority of electors resident in the parish praying that a public inquiry be instituted into the reasons for the dismissal of the teachers, Mr and Mrs Higdon, and whether he was now in a position to state the nature of the reply he proposed to make thereto. . . .

No public inquiry was instituted, but events at Burston had brought home to the Rector and the School Managers that the strike was far more serious than the 'nine days' wonder' they had anticipated. They decided to take matters into their own hands to bring it to an end.

The farmers were not prepared to sack the striking labourers whom they needed for the harvest. Instead they hit upon another plan which caused no inconvenience to themselves and broke with an ancient custom that the villagers had come to regard as sacrosanct. The Rector had at his disposal the distribution of the glebe lands which were rented out at a peppercorn rent to the villagers. Many farm labourers, trying to provide for large families on what amounted to subsistence wages, were only able to do so because they had a piece of glebe land on which they could grow their own produce, fatten a pig, or keep some chickens. The Rector and his clique of farmers decided that the best way to bring the Burston strikers to heel was to threaten to take the glebe land from them. The strikers were appalled at this form of retaliation. Many had rented the same glebe lands for generations and no Rector had ever questioned their rights to the land before. They were not going to be evicted without a fight. Emily Wilby wrote in her account:

> Dismissing Mr and Mrs Higdon is not the only thing the Parson did. He took some Glebe land from three poor men. One of the men was blind; the Parson took his Glebe away because he lent us his shop for a Strike School. He took Mr Harry Ling's Glebe away because he would not let his daughter go to the mock inquiry or go himself to tell a lie. He took Mr Garnham's Glebe away because he attended the Strike School meetings.

We do not know whose idea the eviction scheme was. However, treatment meted out to Ambrose Sandy, who had merely acted as a friend to the Higdons, does seem to have been particularly harsh. As Tom Higdon wrote:

> The Glebe Evictions have already been noted and are still being fought – except in the case of the poor blind man whom circumstances, mainly due to his victimisation, have compelled to leave the village. Had not the Rector taken the glebe meadow away from him he would have purchased the cottage adjacent to it and remained in the village, every inch of which, though blind, he knew by heart and touch.

Ambrose Sandy decided to leave the village before the eviction actually took place. He had probably inherited the carpenter's shop from his mother and rented it out to the Higdons for £3 a year. When he left the village he sold the shop, and the Strike School had to leave. Plans were already going ahead to build a school of their own, and funds were being collected for this purpose. After they left the shop the Higdons put up a shack on the Green, much to the fury of Eland who immediately set about trying to get it taken down. The Higdons then succeeded in buying a plot of land adjacent to the Green and the prefab was transferred to this site until the Strike School was ready for use.

The village was outraged to see Ambrose Sandy go. But worse was to follow from Eland's action against Harry Ling. Both he and his brother William rented pieces of glebe land, at £1 a year for three-quarters of an acre. Harry was the father of Marjory Ling, Violet Potter's best friend at school, and a strong Higdon supporter; his brother, however, was the church sexton and his sister-in-law the infants' teacher at the Council School, which placed them firmly in the opposing camp. The Rector took Harry Ling's land and gave it to William. Marjory Ling remembered when her father first crossed swords with the Rector:

> . . . the parson came into my Father's shop, he was a master shoemaker, . . . and he said would I go and say that this boy was rude to the children in the playground because he knew that we were going to be summonsed and my father said 'No. I've never told a lie in my life,' he said. 'And I'm not going to let my daughters tell a lie, now get off my premises.' And of course after that he had notice to quit the glebe land and that was the start of it all.

Marjory's sister, Florence, described the glebe lands as she remembered them:

> Actually in the beginning it was one big field and it belonged to the vicarage and it was all cut up into pieces. I suppose each of them had three quarters of an acre each and Dad had his next to the house . . .

By giving Harry Ling's glebe land to William, the Rector caused a complete rift between the two sides of the family. Marjory remembered the battles that ensued:

He had notice from the parson that he was to give up this glebe land. He used to grow corn on it, supplied the chickens and things with corn and the straw went to the pigs. . . . He had to give it up and of course the following year my father had this farm at the top of the road, he set the corn. . . . It grew in the spring time, as corn do, to about six or eight inches, when came my uncle with his plough and ploughed it all in and he set it again after that and still the same thing happened, he ploughed it all in and then the schoolmistress said, 'Well, Mr Ling,' she said, 'Put your chickens on there, it is your land' and he put these chickens up and surrounded by wire netting and things like that and someone came and bashed it all down. That's how it went on so of course eventually he couldn't cope with it any more, things were happening like that not in his favour and he gave it all up. . . . One day my cousin came up from the bottom of the field with a pitchfork and he was running up the side of the field and my married sister was at home then and she shouted and we were all standing in the field and my cousin was running up with a pitchfork and he certainly would have put it through my father if my sister hadn't said. He was vicious, all the time.

The bitter hostilities that grew up between the members of the Ling family lasted for a long time. The two brothers did not speak to each other for fifteen years. Besides the persecution from members of his own family, Marjory's father also had to endure ostracism from the local farmers, who were some of his most valuable customers:

You see my father had a fair livelihood in the village, the farmers would bring their repairs to him . . . and they by-passed him. It's ridiculous really when you think of it, why they should boycott him. It was only the strikers that patronised him, you see, and a lot of these people used to do a lot of their own repairs.

In spite of these persecutions, the strikers still remained loyal to the Higdons and the injustice of the glebe evictions strengthened their commitment to the strike. The Rector, meanwhile, continued to take whatever opportunity he could find to punish the parents. Tom Higdon recorded:

Another move of the Rector and his Committee was the dismissal, without notice, of two of the Strike parents from their work of scavenging at the Council School, for which work they had been regularly paid fifteen shillings per quarter – another man now being sent to do the job. The School Caretaker was also threatened with dismissal if she did not send her child back to the Council School, while many other intimidations were attempted. But in all these cases, threats, intimidations, and victimisations alike failed to produce the desired effect and, strange to say, the brave little woman Caretaker continues her work at the Council School to this day, though her child still attends the Strike School. . . .

The Higdons did lose quite a number of their strongest supporters but not as a result of the Rector's tactics. Following the official declaration of war on 4 August 1914, a number of the young men in the village volunteered for the Army. The villagers, torn by their own conflicts, were suddenly swept up in the upheavals that were shaking the whole of Europe.

Chapter 8
A Village at War

When wilt Thou save Thy people,
O, god of Mercy, when?
The people, Lord, the people,
Not thrones and crowns, but men.
Flowers of Thy heart, O God, are they,
Let them not pass like weeds away,
Their heritage a sunless day,
God save the people.
Ebenezer Elliott, The People's Anthem

The Higdons were faced with the one issue on which they were divided. Kitty remained a firm pacifist and hated all talk of the war whereas Tom had always revelled in a fight for what he believed to be a good cause. Although he was too old to enlist, he soon became involved in the war effort. A group of soldiers, believing Tom to be a pacifist, went to beat him up but they arrived to find him holding a recruitment meeting:

> Time and space forbids one to tell of a Recruiting Meeting held at Burston, to which a company of soldiers were invited from Diss by a leading Burston Farmer, one of the Churchwardens, and how some score or so of soldiers came armed with clubs to 'give that – Schoolmaster socks' – as they declared as they passed through the village on their way to the meeting.
>
> A Corporal of the company confessed the whole business to Mr H. a day or two afterwards, and expressed on behalf of his comrades and himself their deep regret for having been misled by their informant, who had, he said, 'let the Skulemaster down to the lowest,' and said that he was opposed to recruiting etc., etc. Thus they had come to the meeting expecting to find the Schoolmaster as an interrupter, instead of which they found him in the chair; for, notwithstanding the presence at the meeting of the Rector of Burston and the Rector of the neighbouring parish of Gissing, the Burston folk assembled would have no one but the 'Skulemaster' to preside over the meeting. The principal organiser of the meeting – a well-known Norwich Socialist – had also fixed upon Mr H. as Chairman of the meeting. Thus the soldiers found no occasion for the use of their clubs. The Churchwarden was not present – for fear of the blows he had hoped to bring down upon other heads than his own.

George Durbidge, Arthur Moore, who was 'walking out' with Violet Potter at this time, and Harry Ling's son, as well as Eland's only son Arthur, were among the band of volunteers who left the village in uniform. But the loss of their loved ones did not help to unite the people of Burston. On 30 October 1914, the *Diss Express* described the heated debate that took place at the Parish Council meeting over the glebe evictions:

Mr Higdon mentioned that one of the tenants of the glebe land (Mr Sandy) had had notice to quit and it was hinted this course was taken because he would not eject him (Mr Higdon) from the Strike School. Mention was also made of similar notices having been served upon people who were associated with what he termed the popular cause in the parish. He afterwards moved the following resolution: 'That this Parish meeting expresses its indignation at the arbitrary and tyrannous methods adopted in giving notice to some old and respected glebe tenants and hopes that means may be found for preventing the effect of such notices'. Mr Joseph Cobb seconded.

In a somewhat heated discussion the Rector told those who were submitting the resolution to mind their own business, and that he should do as he pleased. In reply to a taunt by Mr Higdon, he denied that he had ever written a word, educational or otherwise, against him in that parish, and no proof to the contrary could be produced.

After the motion had been carried, Mr Ling asked the Rector if he would give him a reason why a notice had been served upon him to give up his glebe land. The Rector replied that he should not. Asked if he had always paid his rent an affirmative answer was given. The questioner said that he had hired the land for twenty years, but the Rector replied that had nothing to do with it whatever. Pressed upon the question as to the reason for the notice being given the Rector said it was his business, and he had not treated the questioner differently from others who had been served with notices. He denied that he had acted from prejudice, and added – 'If your landlord chose to give you notice you would be obliged to go out. I have a perfect right to give you notice.' Excitement, which had been at a somewhat high pitch during the proceedings, here became more intense, and an unseemly wrangle ensued, in which offensive epithets were hurled one against the other, personalities were indulged in, and reflections made respecting Church and parochial affairs, the meeting ultimately breaking up in some confusion.

When the villagers appealed to the Bishop of Norwich he wrote that 'if the persons named feel aggrieved they should seek redress through the legal tribunals.' The journalist Casey commented:

So His Lordship, with an income of £4,500 per year, a palace, etc., advises three poor folk, one of whom is blind, to 'seek redress through the legal tribunals'. This be certainly His Lordship's grim joke. How poor folk, waxing lean and keeping families on between £40 and £50 per year, sometimes feasting on bread and lard, whilst glebe owners munch biscuits and cream, can indulge in such luxury as 'The Law' passes what Darby Doyle would call 'the wit av mortial man'.

In fact, the villagers who had had eviction notices served upon them took the more sensible line of holding on to their glebe land and letting the Rector take out proceedings against them. The National Agricultural Labourers' and Rural Workers' Union provided them with a solicitor, who, although he did not succeed in establishing their rights to the land, did put in a successful counter-claim for trespass because the Rector had tried to harass them on their glebe lands before the ejectment order had been passed. The solicitor wrote in his report for 1916:

> Burston Glebe Evictions – Arising out of the famous Burston School Strike, proceedings were taken against your Member and another to eject them from land which they had cultivated for years, and the rent of which they had honourably and punctually paid. The cases were a sad illustration of the lengths to which a landlord may go if he chooses to exercise his powers arbitrarily. The E.C. agreed to share the expense with the other defendant, and it, of course, became my duty to prevent the landlord obtaining an order of ejectment if I could do so. Twice I succeeded in satisfying the magistrates that the landlord had not made out his case, but upon a third hearing additional evidence was found and orders were made.
>
> Subsequently I was instructed by the Union to represent them in actions brought against them for rent. There was no answer to the claims, but I counter-claimed for trespass, the landlord having entered before he got the order of ejectment. Upon those counter-claims it was with great pleasure that I recovered damages.

Tom Higdon believed that the Rector, not satisfied with these evictions, had more ambitious plans:

Of victimisations and evictions there have been no end, yet nothing like so many as there would have been if the Rector could have had his way. It is a well-known fact that the Rector wrote the owner of the cottage, occupied by Mr Noah Sandy with a view to getting Mr Sandy turned out, and that the Rector also asked to be allowed to take over a row of three cottages occupied by Strikers and Strike sympathisers and supporters with a view to turning all these people out. His object from first to last appears to have been to turn by compulsion the whole Parish into a sort of Church Colony of grovelling imbeciles in perfect servility and subserviency to his own despotic and idiotic will.

If this was indeed Eland's intention, he failed dismally, but he did succeed in arousing suspicion and hostility among the villagers.

The depth of this ill-feeling can be gauged from the fight that took place in the church over the memorial tablet to Harry Garnham's son, an early victim of the slaughter being carried on in France. Harry Garnham's brother-in-law put up the tablet in the church without telling the young man's parents. When Garnham heard about it, he went to the church with his daughter Daisy to ask Eland to take it down. As a loyal supporter of the Higdons, he did not want his son's memorial in the Rector's domain. When Eland refused, father and daughter became embroiled in a mêlée in the church itself. Ranged on the Rector's side were Alfred Johnson and his wife, the sexton William Ling and Mrs Eland. The *Norwich Mercury*'s report of 23 June 1917 takes up the story:

Immediately afterwards Mr Garnham stood up and struck the tablet several blows with a coal hammer, but was prevented from doing further damage by the interference of the Rector, Mr Johnson and Mr Ling.

An extraordinary scene ensued. Mr Johnson eventually got hold of Garnham round the waist and pulled him back from the tablet, having after some difficulty got possession of the hammer. While this was being done Miss Daisy Garnham tried to assist her father, and it was alleged that Ling was assaulted by her in trying to prevent him getting the hammer. . . . The tablet, which is affixed to the wall on the south side of the nave, was cracked from the bottom nearly to the top, and several bits of the surface of the marble have been knocked off, while some of the letterpress was also defaced. . . .

Miss Daisy Garnham – 'The Rev. Eland pushed me aside very roughly, but I pushed him back in self-defence. Then there was quite a scrummage and with the assistance of Mrs Johnson and Mrs Eland, Mr Johnson and Mr Ling, they caught hold of me and bruised my arm. I fell down in the struggle, my eye was struck and I got a black eye.' She emphatically denied using strong language.

Mrs Garnham strongly asserted that the tablet had been put in the church by her brother (Mr R. B. Ford) through malice and spite, because her brother could not persuade her husband to discontinue attending strike meetings on the Green. 'I have lived here 27 years,' she said, 'and my husband has never had the law on him until he was turned out of the glebe land. It is,' she continued, 'my determination that this tablet shall come out either by fair means or foul.'

Questioned about what happened to Mr Ling on Sunday afternoon, Mr Garnham said, 'Mr Higdon and my son Charles met Ling near his home. They said they would carry him shoulder high for the good conduct he had shown towards my daughter in church that morning. They picked him up and carried him a few yards. They did not hurt him.

The fight led to summonses and counter-summonses. Everyone had a case against everyone else: Garnham was summonsed for doing wilful and malicious damage to the tablet; Daisy Garnham was summonsed for violent behaviour in church, and with aiding and abetting her father. The Rector, Alfred Johnson, and William Ling were summonsed by Daisy Garnham for assault. T. G. Higdon, Henry Garnham, Ann Marie Garnham, and Daisy Garnham were summonsed for having used abusive and insulting language to the Rev. C. T. Eland and Mrs Eland on 1 July 1917.

The court proceedings proved to be an emotional affair. After Henry Garnham had been sentenced to one month's imprisonment with hard labour, and Daisy Garnham had been bound over to keep the peace for a year, Daisy, her mother, and the accompanying family of Garnhams all burst into tears. Mr Higdon, to save Garnham from gaol, declared that he would willingly pay £20 or go to prison himself, but the Chairman insisted that the case had been settled. Higdon and the Garnhams were fined £1 for the assault on William Ling, although Henry Garnham claimed that they had given him a joyride.

On 10 October 1917, an appeal against Garnham's imprisonment was heard at Norfolk Quarter Sessions and his sentence was modified to imprisonment only. A protest meeting was held on Burston Green at which, according to a local newspaper report:

> ... T. G. Higdon claimed that the Rector and churchwardens had broken the law by allowing the tablet to be erected in the church without a faculty and that Garnham by his action had really upheld the law. He protested against Garnham being imprisoned for carrying out what he believed to be only a parental duty. Mr George Perrement, of Norwich, contended if the working classes had been represented on the Magisterial Bench, such a sentence would never have been imposed. No resolution was submitted to the meeting. During the proceedings Daisy Garnham was called forward and handed the sum of 30s.4d, the amount of a collection taken on Garnham's behalf.

The fierce struggles over the glebe land brought home to the villagers that their rights were ignored by those in authority. Realising that they had no protection from church or state, the Burston labourers became more insistent on a fair wage. With the scarcity of labour, owing to the war, and the need for increased home production, they found themselves in a more powerful position than they had ever been before. The farmers needed their labour and, if they chose to strike, there was no longer a supply of unemployed or part-time workers, as there had been in the pre-war years, to take their place. In his report for the year ending 31 December 1914, the General Secretary of the National Agricultural Labourers' and Rural Workers' Union wrote:

> In the Spring an effort was put forth to secure an advance in wages, etc. for our members in Norfolk, with the result that 1/- a week was secured without having to adopt the weapon of a strike. The standard weekly wage in the County was now 15/- and as high as ever wages have been in the days of Arch.

Chapter 9
'A Hall of Freedom'

Oh, I love this old huz of a world –
I can't help it – I love her!
I love her much better than Heaven
Far away and above her.

I love her! – I love what is real:
I am not a dreamer. –
She is sinful I know – not too black
For love to redeem her.

Oh I love the old huzzy I do –
So wicked and good!
Deceitful, she's honest with me,
I know her old blood.

She is more than a mother to me –
Than a maiden's her charms;
What tokens and gifts she bestows
With her bountiful arms! . . .

. . . She is Mortal – alas! and she knows it –
When pales her complexion;
But my dust she will mingle with hers
Till the last resurrection –

When I fear me the great consummation
Will rend her to pieces –
That the end of the world will be ending
Both her and my species.

Tom Higdon, Of the Earth – Earthy

Twenty-three new branches of the Union were opened in the first year of the war at Dersingham, Blofield, Mattishall, Docking, Bradenham, Erpingham, Boughton, Hevingham and fifteen other places in Norfolk. Events at Burston may have brought home to those in the neighbouring villages that collective bargaining was the only way forward and that they would have to rely on their own strength. In 1915 the General Secretary reported a rise of 3s. in Norfolk, bringing the wages up to 18s. a week. By the end of 1916 they were up to 22s. a week.

The Burston Strike was also a triumphant demonstration of a change of attitude. The Higdons had helped to give the villagers a new sense of confidence. They discovered they could stand up for their rights, challenge authority, expect a fair wage for a fair day's work and look forward to a better future for their children. The Higdons were not just do-gooders; they had a vision which they shared with the people of Burston. George Bourne in his *Journals* came close to expressing what the Higdons must have thought and felt:

> I think English men and women have it in them to be something better than peasants; and indeed, we are beginning to know it. That standard is too humble and narrow a one, for men of this fine breed (for we *are* a fine breed). I desire to be able to judge my fellow countrymen, and to approve them, not as good peasants, but as good well-developed human beings. . . .
>
> I claim, and many with me are claiming, a full varied development for the English. And the English are not many years distant from claiming something of the sort for themselves. Somehow the layers that were above them have worn thin. The unknown people are beginning to feel themselves near the surface, where, besides getting a living, they may live it worthily. Believe me, as I go about the roads and look at them, I feel that release is very near indeed, and I am gladdened by the immense riches of character, legible in people's faces and manners. Just another generation or two of ambitious thought (thought ambitious for the true success of Englishness) and then there may be a magical change, the English coming to new life, after so many centuries.

New ideas take root slowly, especially in country districts, and

Tom Higdon was disappointed that his colleagues in the Union were not prepared to press for more widespread reforms:

> ... When the trouble arose at Burston the blood of the labourers, not only at Burston but over a very wide area, and, indeed throughout Norfolk generally, was up, and had the officials of the Labourers' Union given the rank and file a lead in the matter the fight would have been a big one – a fight involving all the fundamentals, issues and opportunities of Rural Trade Unionism for which the Union stands. The Burston School Strike has certainly shown the way, and by so doing has come into tangible grip with all the petty tyrannies, oppressions, religious hypocrisies, individual and class privileges which exist in the country districts. Though the inhabitants of other villages flocked to Burston on Sundays no attempt was made to carry the fight to their doors, consequently this greater upheaval did not take definite shape. ...

The Burston Strike may not have caused the 'greater upheaval' Tom Higdon had hoped for, but it certainly caused a stir in socialist circles. Fund-raising meetings were held in London, and Burston continued as a place of pilgrimage for leading figures in the movement. As the years passed, the villagers got to know the leading socialist figures of their time. Marjory Ling remembered a visit from Sylvia Pankhurst. She went to tea at the Lings' home and admired Marjory's mother's Nottingham lace curtains:

> There was Mrs Pankhurst, Miss Pankhurst she had to go upstairs and of course we hadn't the facilities they have now to wash her hands and mother gave her some water and she washed her hands upstairs and she said 'Oh Mrs Ling,' she said, 'what wonderful clean curtains you have here, so white' and mother says 'Well,' she said, 'That's how I like them'. In London, she said, when they hung theirs for a little while they would be black. ...

The Higdons encouraged all the Burston families who could do so to entertain the visitors in their homes so they were able to meet and talk and exchange ideas. Most colourful and memorable of all were the meetings patronised by members of other unions who gave the strikers both moral and financial support. Marjory's sister remembered:

> . . . some wonderful meetings on the green and they used to come down, the miners and the railwaymen, and they had these big banners, huge banners, with beautiful coloured silks and all the gold tassels, it took a couple of men each side to carry the banners, come off the station and march through the village, you've never seen anything like it. And then of course they held all these meetings and the money just poured in and then that's how this school strike was made. . . . I don't know where the schoolmistress got these books of all the addresses in . . . but I know that she had these leaflets printed and she gave us, all the senior ones, a job addressing these to the different places you see and that's how the money came in you see. . . .

As usual, the local press was on hand to report the meetings. On 4 December 1917, the *Norwich Mercury* carried the following account:

> The village of Burston was the scene on Sunday of one of the most remarkable sights and demonstrations which ever took place in a rural village, when some 200 NUR union branch officials and delegates from London, Colchester, Ipswich, Southsea, Bury St Edmunds, Norwich, Beccles, Diss and other places attended with handsome silk banners representing their various branches, and marched through the village, finally forming up in a picturesque crescent upon the village green, where a meeting was held upon the frozen grass, followed throughout by hundreds of deeply interested people assembled from Burston, Diss, and district, the gathering being presided over by Mr Higdon, on whose behalf, and that of Mrs Higdon, the demonstration had been arranged.

There was a unanimous vote for the resolution:

> That this mass meeting of railwaymen, agricultural labourers and vehicle workers, representing 50,000 workers, protests against the unjust dismissal of Mr and Mrs Higdon and the attempted eviction of two glebe tenants by the Rector of Burston, and calls the Board of Education and the Norfolk

Education Committee to grant a public inquiry with a view to the reinstatement of the teachers.

A Strike School fund was set up and eventually over £1000 was collected. This sum enabled the Higdons to buy a piece of land and build a school of their own on the edge of the Green. The school could now look forward to leaving the wooden building that had temporarily housed them since Ambrose Sandy's enforced departure from the village. On 17 May 1917 George Lansbury laid the foundation stone for the new school. A large contingent of supporters came up from London to celebrate including Sylvia Pankhurst, who described the day's events in *The Woman's Dreadnought*. Her words give us a final view of a defeated Eland, now only an embittered onlooker at the Higdons' day of triumph. She recalled how the Londoners, escorted by Mr Carter, one of the main organisers of the demonstration and treasurer of the Burston School Fund, were greeted at Burston station:

> The train was nearing Burston – a cottage roof or two, a line of trees in the distance, was all that one could see; it seemed almost too small to be a village. But this was Burston Station, and soon Mr Carter was marshalling us in the lane. The men of the Bethnal Green NUR band, out to play for the first time, were taking the covers from their brass instruments; eighteen or twenty great painted silk banners, gorgeous in brilliant red and green and blue and purple and gleaming gold and silver, were being unfurled and hoisted. Their huge size seemed to dwarf everything about us, even the old trees. Parties with banners still furled came down the road to meet us: contingents from Norwich and the surrounding district, and Londoners who had reached Burston the night before. Then came the Burston people; children in clean, white Sunday frocks, women waiting for our approach and hurrying towards us, some of them bent with toil, but all with shining faces; . . . By twos and threes they joined us. We marched joyously, big banners swaying and bearers staggering a little under them, and guiding them carefully away from the branches of the trees. And amongst all the other banners was the big new one of the Agricultural Labourers' Union – unfurled today.

At the church gate we met the parson, sallow and thin and small in his black dress. Everyone looked at him. There was a little hooting, mainly from the children, but for the most part curiosity made us dumb. . . .

But as we reached the Green all troubles were forgotten. There was the old carpenter's shop which first housed the strike school. Here was the temporary wooden structure erected for the scholars when they were obliged to leave the carpenter's shop, and used until now. And there, all new and sharp-cut, with its windows yet unglazed, and woodwork yet unpainted, was the new Strike School. Its stones are graven with the names of the societies which have subscribed towards its erection: Miners' lodges, NUR and other Trade Union branches, branches of the ILP, BSP, N-CF, and so on, in England, Scotland and Wales. A tablet by the doorpost tells the story:

'Mr T. G. Higdon and Mrs A. K. Higdon were unjustly dismissed from the Council School of this village on the 31st day of March, 1914. This building was erected by public subscription, to protest against the action of the Education Authorities, to provide a free school, to be a centre of rural democracy and a memorial to the villagers' fight for freedom . . .'

A thousand people assembled on the green to hear Violet Potter say: 'With love and thankfulness I open this school to be a hall of freedom,' and to see her lead in the fifty little scholars.

The Strike School still stands on Burston Green today.

The Burston Strike School lasted for 25 years, from 1914 until the outbreak of the Second World War. In 1950 the School was reopened as a social and educational centre and remains so at the present time.

The Higdons lived at Burston for the rest of their lives and are buried side by side in the village churchyard. The Rev. Charles Tucker Eland left Burston a few years after the Strike and went to another parish at Sawtry, near Peterborough. He died in Eastbourne at the age of 67.

Bertram Edwards, author of The Burston School Strike, published in 1974, which sadly is now out of print, has kept up with many of the Higdons' old pupils whom he met in the course of his research. His epilogue gives an account of what has happened to the school and the main characters involved in the Strike and describes how he first discovered the story and found himself following in the Higdons' footsteps along the road from Diss to Burston.

Epilogue

The Burston story first caught my attention early in 1971. I had taken a group of friends to see *Captain Swing at the Penny Gaff*, a play about the agricultural unrest in the southern counties in 1830, produced at the Unity Theatre, in the script of which I had been involved. During the interval I went out into the foyer to browse around the exhibition of books and pamphlets set up by the National Union of Agricultural and Allied Workers. Reg Groves's *Sharpen the Sickle*, a short history of the Union, was on show and I bought a copy.

At home I found the book compulsive reading and when I finally put it down I could not get the chapter on 'The Burston School Strike' out of my mind. For one thing I was ashamed of my ignorance. I had been a member of the National Union of Teachers for over twenty years, and I had never even heard of the Burston School Strike.

Groves's story filled me with admiration for the Higdons. I was suddenly aware that my faith in humanity had been rekindled, and I determined to find out more about them. On 16 October 1971, I went by train to Diss and walked to Burston along the same route that Kitty and Tom had taken on 31 January 1911. Tom Potter was expecting me and we talked, and then he led me across the Green and I stood in fascination outside the Strike School, looking at the names and initials on the façade. Inside the building I was deeply moved by the evidence of the Higdons' occupation long ago, the large picture of Daniel in the Lions' Den on the wall, the framed photograph of George Edwards above the left-hand fireplace, the shield presented by the Bermondsey Branch of the NUR, the board showing the names of the first children on the Strike School roll.

As my notes, documents, press-cuttings, and photographs about the strike accumulated, I became more and more astonished that the story was so little heard of, more and more determined to make it known. After two years' research I wrote a book which, after many rejections, was finally accepted by Lawrence & Wishart in 1973. About this time, quite coincidentally, the Burston School Strike was brought to the attention of Stephen Peet, then producing the *Yesterday's Witness* programmes on BBC2. He decided to base a programme on the story, and I was able to help with much of the background material. The programme was shown in 1974, four months after my book had reached the bookstalls, and later, Stephen Peet sent me photocopies of two letters he had received from nieces of Tom Higdon, one living in Buckhurst Hill, Essex, the other in Wells, Somerset. I went to see them both and was able to borrow and copy two small books of his poems which I had heard about but had not yet seen.

With the help of some of the villagers I arranged a get-together of Wood Dalling and Burston folk who had been pupils of the Higdons long ago. After tea in the Strike School we went in procession round to the Chapel and sang some of Kitty's favourite hymns to an accompaniment on the American organ which she had presented to the Chapel when she closed the School in 1939. 'However can I thank you enough', Violet Potter wrote, 'for the Reunion Party yesterday and for all you have done to bring this about, as it's through you this has all come to life again. . . . It was lovely to see old faces again. . . .'

Other events followed that have helped to ensure that the story of the Burston School Strike will not be forgotten. In April 1977, documents given to me by some of the villagers and others were handed over to the Norfolk Records Office at a public ceremony in the Central Library, Norwich, before a gathering that included twenty ex-pupils of the Higdons. Then, in May 1978, a dedication ceremony was held in Burston Churchyard, attended by a dozen ex-pupils, when a headstone to mark Kitty's grave was put up next to Tom's which had been refaced.

By 1983 the trade union movement was becoming interested in the idea of re-starting the annual rallies that used to take place on Burston Green in the 1920s and 1930s. In the meantime the Strike School Trustees, beset by the expense of the upkeep of the historic building and the paramount need to preserve it for future generations, were planning a 70th Anniversary Appeal for £30,000. The Transport and General Workers' Union and the Trustees agreed to work together to organise a rally for September 1984, the primary aim of which should be the appeal for funds for the Strike School. On the basis of the developing support the Trustees undertook the republication of Tom Higdon's *Burston Rebellion*. Maurice Philpot, Trustee and Treasurer, saw the book through the press and the job was done.

I had always wanted to see a dramatisation of the story, and this dream was realised when I went to see a special viewing of the BBC television drama *The Burston Rebellion* in February 1985. About a dozen of those who had been involved in the story were there, and they were delighted to see Kitty and Tom Higdon accurately portrayed by Eileen Atkins and Bernard Hill and proud to feel that they had played a part in such a historic event. This book is yet another step towards spreading the Burston story, and I hope that this remarkable event will soon be recognised, along with the story of Tolpuddle, as one of the great developments in the fight for independence of the rural working man.

At the author's request I have added a few notes about the later story of the Strike School and about the Higdons and some of their former pupils and friends still living in the village.

Bertram Edwards, June 1985

The Strike School

The Strike School continued until the Second World War when Tom Higdon died and Mrs Higdon, now in her seventies, was unable to carry on alone.

In a fund-raising leaflet of 30 May 1919, she had written:

The School Strike which began on April 1st, 1914, has now been in existence over five years and has thus seen the War in and out, and still the parents, children and teachers and their supporters in Burston are solidly united in their protest against injustice and tyranny and in their fight for Freedom.

Many of the scholars who first came out on strike have, of course, left the school and gone to work, but forty children are still attending the Strike School, and such is the hold of this new democratic, educational and social movement upon the life of the village that most of the infants who come along find their way to the Strike School to take the places of the older children who are constantly leaving. Thus what began as a strike of school children on behalf of their teacher and was spoken of by the Rector Chairman of the School Managers as 'all moonshine', 'a nine days' wonder', etc., has become a permanent Socialist Educational Cause and Institution, or as our comrade 'Casey' says, 'the first Trade Union School in England'.

After she closed down the school in 1939 the building was used for meetings and social events. But it is interesting to record that Mrs Louise Moore, whom I interviewed many times, said, 'our eldest son, and the next eldest, got on all right, even at the end. They were transferred to the Council School. There were eleven of them left who were transferred when the School was closed. In fact, I think our two got on better at the Strike School than they did at the Council School afterwards.'

The present Burston Strike School Trustees are hoping to renovate the building to keep it as a memorial and museum of the Strike which can still be used as a meeting place for the people of Burston.

Tom Higdon

Tom Higdon remained an active member of the Agricultural Labourers' Union and continued to teach at the Strike School until shortly before his death in 1939. He was Treasurer of the Union from 1916 to 1920, and on the Executive Committee from 1914 to 1938, apart from a break between 1924 and 1927. As County Secretary, for many years, he cycled hundreds of miles annually on Union business. In 1923 he was on the County Emergency

Committee conducting the four-week strike in Norfolk for the Union. The *Diss Express* reported, on 6 April 1923, a ninth Anniversary Meeting on Burston Green, presided over 'by Tom Higdon who spoke at some length on the farm strike. A novel feature was the naming, at an after-meeting, of three babies, in lieu of the usual christening. This little ceremony was performed by Miss Sylvia Pankhurst on the Green. . . .'

Tom was a member of the Management Committee of the Diss Co-operative Society, a member of the Independent Labour Party, and an active Depwade Rural District Councillor. His passionate commitment to social justice remained unabated. A local paper gave an account on 12 August 1938 of a Depwade UDC meeting at which a Report of the Rural Housing Conference held at Bury St Edmunds was considered. In a long and heated argument Tom Higdon violently 'opposed the idea of grants to farmers for the building of houses that will be tied cottages. . . .' Another report, on 20 August 1937, gives an idea of the depth of his convictions on this issue after a family had been evicted from a farm cottage in Burston.

> Mr and Mrs Tom Higdon, the teachers of the Strike School, are championing the unfortunate family. Mr Higdon is reported to have said: 'We are allowing the family to have temporary shelter here. It is the only thing between them and the Workhouse. This eviction is the most unjust, outrageous, and barbarous thing possible in these days of supposed advanced civilisation, and how any Bench of Magistrates could allow it to happen passes comprehension.'

Arthur Moore, who left the Strike School in 1913, said of Tom Higdon that he was: '. . . one of the straightest men I've ever come across. He was a good living man.'

Kitty Higdon

Few of Kitty Higdon's pupils ever forgot the emphasis that she gave in her teaching to Christian principles, courage and compassion. During the strike of 1926 six miners' children were lodged in the village and attended the Strike School and one of them stayed with the Higdons until he left school and joined the merchant navy.

Tom Potter, Violet's younger brother, remembers two boys from the Soviet Trade Delegation lodging with the Higdons and attending the Strike School. It was their fathers who presented Mr Higdon with the large picture of Daniel in the Lions' Den which still hangs in the school.

For many years Kitty Higdon and the Strike School were the very heart of the village. Inevitably, as time passed this heart beat less strongly. G. C. T. Giles, the London headmaster who later became President of the National Union of Teachers, had sent his sons to the school in the 1920s. As she grew older, he tried to persuade Kitty to take on an assistant. 'She just wouldn't listen. We drove around in a trap for hours and got nowhere. She was old and obstinate. It was *her* school.'

Win Potter (née Leeder) recalled, 'Mrs Higdon was heartbroken when Tom died. His body was not taken into the church. He was taken into the Strike School. It was crowded to overflowing with personal and trade union friends. Mrs Higdon knelt down by the coffin and sang beautifully. The coffin was brought to the Strike School on a farm cart, provided by 'Fetchum' Potter, Tom's father. It was driven by Stanley Potter, Tom's brother. Violet Turner (née Potter) was there. 'The Strike School was crowded. Mrs Higdon sang "The Lord is my Shepherd", and everyone was very moved. Many were in tears.'

Left alone, Kitty declined. Several times she was found wandering in the lanes at night, saying that she was waiting for Tom to return home from a union meeting. On one occasion she met Violet and asked her politely whether she was 'coming to school'.

She spent her last days in a home in Swainsthorpe, near Norwich, and died in 1946. Her coffin was brought to Burston on a trailer, her story largely forgotten in the village.

Violet Potter

Violet Potter, who had been the main spirit in organising the strike and became, with Marjory Ling, one of Kitty's young assistants, left Burston in 1918 and went to live with friends in Forest Gate whom she and her mother had met when they visited London in 1916 to attend the public meetings in support of the school organised by the National Union of Railwaymen. She got a job as a ledger clerk in an office in Stratford, East London, but came back to Burston in 1920 when she was twenty, and married at the age of 21. Her husband was a cowman and worked for several farmers before he and Violet took over the Crown Inn at Burston, which they ran for sixteen years. He died soon after they left the Crown, when he was working at Buckenham, as a miller. Three of their children went to the Strike School. Two of them were still of school age when their father died at the early age of 54.

Violet was a keen church worker and a lively participant in all sorts of social activities for pensioners until very near the end of her life. She loved letter-writing, and correspondence with Violet was one of the delights of my long research into the Burston story. She died in 1979.

Tom Potter

Violet Potter's brother, Tom, was born in 1914 and was christened on the Green by John Sutton, the Methodist lay preacher. He and his younger brother, George, were both named after Tom (T. G.) Higdon. George, also, was christened on the Green. Their father, John Potter, known in the village as 'Fetchum', became a small tenant farmer in the early twenties. The third brother, Stan, carried on the farm with Tom when their father died.

Tom remained in farming until he took over the Post Office Stores in the village in 1961. He runs it still, with his wife, Elsie. He has been an active District and Parish Councillor for many years.

Arthur Moore

Arthur Moore was a pupil at the Council School in 1911 when the Higdons arrived in Burston and he left school at the age of thirteen to work on the land. His wage was 4s a week, the adult wage at this time being 13s. He joined the Union in 1914, when the Burston branch was formed. In 1930 he became branch secretary and held this post until 1970.

He used to cycle to Union meetings with Tom Higdon and forty years after his death he retains a deep love and admiration for him. He still lives in Burston.

Sol Sandy

Sol Sandy is the son of Noah Sandy who asked Tom Higdon to stand for election at the Annual Parish Meeting in 1913. He was born in 1895 and had left school when the Higdons arrived from Wood Dalling. He has a remarkable memory of village life at the turn of the century. He attended many of the meetings on the Green and remembers the prominent people who came to Burston, Philip Snowden, George Lansbury, A. J. Cook, Tom Mann, and many others.

He joined his father and his brother Noah in their jobbing building trade when he left school, and served in the Royal Engineers on the railways, in France, during the First World War. After the war he lodged for a time in Ipswich and worked on the railway there. Eventually he came back to Burston and became a smallholder and worked odd days for local farmers. It is Sol Sandy who saved so much of the documentary evidence of the Strike that puts this remarkable story on such a firm foundation.

Selected Reading List

J. Arch, *Joseph Arch: The Story of His Life* (Hutchinson, 1898)

George Bourne, *Change in the Village* (Penguin County Library, 1984)

John Burnett, *Plenty and Want: A Social History of Diet in England from 1815 to the Present Day* (Scolar Press, 1979)

Bertram Edwards, *The Burston School Strike* (Lawrence and Wishart, 1974)

T. G. Higdon, *The Burston Rebellion* (Trustees of the Burston Strike School, 1984)

Pamela Horn, *Joseph Arch (1826–1919) – The Farm Workers' Leader* (Kineton: The Roundwood Press, 1971)

Alun Howkins, *Poor Labouring Men: Rural Radicalism in Norfolk 1872–1923* (History Workshop Series, Routledge and Kegan Paul, 1985)

Stephen Humphries, *Hooligans or Rebels? An Oral History of Working Class Childhood and Youth 1889–1939* (Basil Blackwell, 1981)

W. E. Minchinton, *Essays in Agrarian History, Vols 1 & 2* (David and Charles, 1968)

Christabel S. Orwin and Edith H. Whetham, *History of British Agriculture 1846–1914* (David and Charles, 1971)

Hugh Owen, Jnr, *The Elementary Education Acts, 1870, 1873, etc* (Knight & Co., 1874)

Neil Philip, ed., *Between Earth and Sky* (Penguin Country Library, 1984)

H. Rider Haggard, *A Farmer's Year. Being his Commonplace Book for 1898* (Longmans, Green, & Co., 1899)

——, *Rural England Vols 1 & 2* (Longmans, Green, & Co., 1906)

Raphael Samuel, *Village Life and Labour* (History Workshop Series, Routledge & Kegan Paul, reprinted 1982)

Harold Silver, *Robert Owen on Education – Selections edited with an introduction and notes* (Cambridge University Press, 1969)
Brian Simon, *Education and the Labour Movement 1870–1920* (Lawrence and Wishart, 1965)
Denys Thompson, *Change and Tradition in Rural England – An Anthology of Writings on Country Life* (Cambridge University Press, 1980)
T. G. Williams, *The Main Currents of Social and Industrial Change 1870–1924* (Sir Isaac Pitman and Sons, 1925)